Adam & Eve

Marriage Secrets from the Garden of Eden

Adam & Eve

Marriage Secrets from the Garden of Eden

Michael Shevack

PAULIST PRESS

New York/Mahwah, N.J.

Cover design by Lynn Else

Book design by Celine Allen

Library of Congress Cataloging-in-Publication Data

Shevack, Michael.
  Adam & Eve : marriage secrets from the Garden of Eden / Michael Shevack.
    p. cm.
  ISBN 0-8091-4117-5
  1. Bible. O.T. Genesis I-III—Criticism, interpretation, etc. 2. Marriage—Biblical teaching. 3. Spouses—Religious life. I. Title: Adam and Eve. II. Title.
  BS1238.M37 S54 2003
  248.4—dc21

                          2002153725

Published by Paulist Press
997 Macarthur Boulevard
Mahwah, New Jersey 07430

www.paulistpress.com

Printed and bound in the United States of America

To my wife, Teddy,
whom God fashioned as my helpmate.

CONTENTS

ACKNOWLEDGMENTS

This is a big event in my life. My first book written by me alone. So, I hope you don't mind a little over-indulgence of additional acknowledgements to:

My kids, Christian, Adam, and Zoe, my *real* legacy. Rabbi Jack Bemporad, of the Center for Christian-Jewish Understanding, my "nursing father." Mike McKenna, who introduced me to my agent, Jacques de Spoelberch, who believes in me, a lot. My editor Christopher Bellitto, whom God sent to guide me, knowing I needed it. Phil Dusenberry, Chairman of BBDO North America, who taught me pride. The late Dr. Bryant Kirkland, of Fifth Avenue Presbyterian, who gave me hope. The late John Cardinal O'Connor, for his kind words and support. Chiara Lubich, founder of the Focolare Movement, and Sharry Silvi and Julian Ciabattini, U.S. Directors, who made me believe in Unity. Professor Ellis Rivkin of Hebrew Union College for his unity-principle, his love, and for his wife, Zelda Rivkin, who taught me in one short sentence what women want. My friend, Monsignor Luigi Giussani, founder of Communion and Liberation, whose book *The Religious Sense* heals. Rabbi Joseph Gelberman for his vision of love. Rav and Karen Berg and Esther Sibilia, for being lights of Kabbalah. The Reverends Wade Adkisson and Angie Weber of the Church of Religious Science, my cheerleaders. My Torah study group from Kehillat Ha-Nahar, who taught me the limits of ego. Dioro Boisseau, my counselor. Rev. Joyce Meyer, whose brilliant fundamentalism jolted me out of fear. Maharishi Mahesh Yogi, for his gift to the world. Meyer Baba, for his silence. Guru Mai and Baba Muktananda, who teach peace. Reverend-to-be Carl Christianson, who feels the Lord aright. Dean Dobbins, who keeps my books balanced. Vincent Sebastian Taschetti, my soul-brother. William Ford Jr., CEO of Ford Motors, who sees the future. My pen pal John Randolph Price, who teaches that the impossible is true. Geraldine Hale, who taught me to respect the earth, and myself. Patricia Erceg, Ron Maltz, and Paul Stratton, DC's, who straightened me out. Elizabeth Stratton, M.S.W., who warned me not to pick. Dr. Frank DiBennardo for his ability to listen. John Blackburn, Leah Ruth Robinson, and Marty Hoffman, my teachers. Henry Kornhauser and Alan Yarnoff, my lifesavers. Dennis-Paul and Gary Bennet, with thanks for their Ballyraine Institute, a respected part of the world of human dialogue. Chuck Kent and Christine Marshall, angels who fell too close to earth. My grandparents, parents, brother Brett and sister Debbi, nieces and nephews, aunts, uncles and cousins, friends, including Jeffrey Hollander, Michael Feuer, Ronald Hartenbaum, Ian Bukzin, Larry–The Hugman, Gerald Gordon—and countless others who generously forgive me for not remembering to name them.

Last but first, God, who made them all.

PREFACE

I often feel like an idiot standing in a clerical robe preparing to marry some couple. I feel that way because many consider me some kind of expert merely by virtue of that robe. They often don't look underneath to see the real man, whose knees are knocking together.

An expert in marriage? I don't believe there is one. To my mind, anyone who claims to be an expert in marriage would have to be instantly disqualified.

After all, marriage is a mystery. It is the mystery of the human soul. Is there anyone who fully understands the mystery of the human soul? Can you learn that completely in any Ph.D. program or seminary? If one soul is a cosmic mystery, now just imagine doubling it. That's a mystery of mysteries!

So, please, disqualify me right now from being considered an expert in marriage. I have been married twenty years to the same amazing lady, and in the course of those years I've stumbled, bumbled, and made an absolute fool of myself. I've done things that are so wrong, even cruel, to my wife Teddy that I'm appalled by myself when I look backwards. Each morning I wake up, I start a new day, and

I still, like a toddler tripping over fallen knickers, make mind-boggling errors in my marriage.

Perhaps this is what might actually qualify me as an expert after all. I've made so many mistakes and have had such frequent, mortifying opportunities to reflect upon them, that at least I can teach from experience. I know what *not* to do. In marital mistakes, I'm definitely an expert and, I dare say, I'm not alone.

Yet, after so many years "practicing" marriage—for it requires so much practice—I've begun to put together a semblance of what makes a good marriage, a successful marriage, a happy marriage, a marriage that works on all levels—spiritually, emotionally, psychologically, materially, interpersonally, and sexually.

"It's so simple," I now declare. "Why didn't I realize it before?" Maybe the reason is because I was looking in the wrong place. Like the original Adam, I had fallen into a deep sleep.

Like most of us, I was looking at the model of marriage to which most people in the world adhere. I learned how to behave in marriage by, like a child, mirroring the fallen behaviors of others around me, whether parents, relatives, or friends. I was weaned on re-runs of "I Love Lucy," which are not unlike the story of the Garden of Eden: a conniving Eve who was always trying to manipulate Adam, who, in turn, was totally self-absorbed and unaware of her needs. Yet, I was also weaned on re-runs of "Leave It to Beaver," where Ward and June behaved so perfectly (he even wore a tie to dinner every night) that I actually believed that such a "realistic" couple was real. In between Ricky and Lucy and

Ward and June is a veritable chasm into which so many of us tumble. It's led this present generation to an epidemic in which more than 50 percent of marriages fail.

What's a perfect marriage? Does anyone know? Is there a decent, thorough "marriage guide" out there?

Then, one day, after years of personally struggling to find an approach to marriage that combined both traditional and contemporary values and finally succeeding—well, at least somewhat—I happened to re-read the story of Adam and Eve. My mouth flew open. There it was—right there—disguised in ancient language, but there nonetheless: all the secrets I had stumbled and bumbled to learn, condensed in a tightly woven, spiritually intriguing tale—the very first story of the Bible.

I read about Adam's mistake, and recognized my own and my wife's: I had succumbed to Eve's temptation, as she had succumbed to mine. I felt I actually knew the serpent personally; I knew him as an inner aspect of my own contaminated spiritual make-up. I began to understand, from experience, why we had made a terrible, terrible mistake, taking a nibble of the fruit of the Tree of Knowledge. The meaning of the tale opened up before me like a smorgasbord catered by God.

There, in the first three chapters of the Bible, was the best marriage guide I have ever found. Why hadn't I seen it before? Such a fool, I was. Alas, sometimes we can see things only when we are ready to see them. Until then, I had been reading the story for "religious purposes," thinking through complex issues like "free will," "original sin," "goodness," and "evil"—all very impersonal theological matters. I forgot that all these were woven into the tale for very personal purposes: to teach each of us, male and female, men and women, and not necessarily in that order, how to be married; to present all the spiritual pitfalls of marriage in a few short chapters.

No degreed therapist, priest, minister, or rabbi could have been so succinct. But, then again, the Being who inspired scripture had an eternal amount of training.

There is no expert in marriage except God. After all, God is the only one who could possibly understand the mystery of a single soul, let alone two souls living together as husband and wife.

So I humbly—very, very humbly—present this book to you. I feel even greater humility before my wife, whom I put through so much turmoil in "learning the ropes." She knew a lot more than I, but my ears, like the ears of so many of my fellow Adams, were plugged with male ego.

I've attempted to alternate male and female pronouns as much as possible in order to avoid ungrammatical or awkward wording. Sometimes I simply alternated he and him in one paragraph with she and her in the next. The point to keep in mind is that all of these observations, examples, and secrets can apply to both husbands and wives, regardless of where and which pronouns are used.

Marriage is joyful, wonderful, spontaneous, and spiritually powerful. It is the most delicious and amazing of humanly divine experiences—if you discover the secrets and learn a few basic lessons from them.

They're the same lessons the original couple had to learn. No more. No less.

INTRODUCTION

It wasn't too long ago that the feminist movement began, and the relationship of today's Adam and Eve turned upside down.

Eve decided she was no longer going to be submissive to Adam. She had a right to her own independent thinking, her own viewpoint, and her own accomplishments. She was no longer going to be controlled by her desire for Adam. She was no longer going to be a mere instrument for the painful bearing of Adam's children. Eve was going to be her own person separate from Adam. In essence, Eve had liberated herself from the ancient biblical curse of Eden.

The ancient fall was over. A new climb was to begin, not just for Eve, but for Adam as well. Both would have to learn a new way to be, as individuals and as a married couple.

However, after centuries of males and females locked in rigid roles, uncrossable lines of gender, immutable lines of power, one-way sexual satisfaction, and seemingly unalterable "God-given" standards of "normalcy" for males and females, Eve's liberation has brought about a good deal of spiritual confusion for both.

Today, thank God, Eve is not so under-the-thumb of Adam. But now, unfortunately, we see a different kind of enslavement of Eve. Today's Eve is often thrust into the role of "super-woman." She's not just commanding the kitchen, but is a captain of industry as well, competing with Adam for status and wealth. She often finds herself doing double the work just to have a half-share of Adam's domain. No wonder early heart attacks, once an exclusive male pre-rogative, are now shared as a woman's "right."

Today's Adam often finds himself split as well. He may take to beating drums in male-identity groups or, alterna-tively, seek the instant potency of Viagra. Since today's Eve rebelled, today's Adam has been confused about "what women want," and this has made him confused about what he should be as a man. As a result, we see many an Adam staying an eternal adolescent, hopping from Eve to Eve, fearful, despite years of living together, of making a final commitment. The result of this has been detrimental to Eve, who, having wasted her youth with no commitment, is often pushed against her biological clock, ultimately forced into medical intervention so that she can satisfy her need to have a child—even when, because of her age, pregnancy entails a high risk.

Despite the tremendous freedom in today's more liber-ated Garden, Adam and Eve are still cursed—only in more convoluted forms. Today's Adams and Eves seem to be caught between worlds. They are freer and more educated and have greater options for self-expression. Yet the core, basic, earthly relationship between them as males and females still seems to be standing on shaky ground.

Today's Adams and Eves desperately need to express their freedom in a way that strengthens their marriages rather than undermines them. Today's Adams and Eves need a foundation to their marriage that won't change with the whims of society. They need to build their lives on something more solid than what is fashionable or politically correct for men and women. Today's Adams and Eves, no less than their biblical ancestors, need to build a spiritual foundation for their relationship. To help them do so is the purpose of this book.

What is a natural man?

What is a natural woman?

What is a natural marriage?

What IS natural, anyway?

These are the questions that have been on the minds of men and women for millennia. These are the questions that are still on the minds of today's Adams and Eves, especially with all the intense, even gender-bending options available for today's couples. These are also the questions that the story of Adam and Eve answers.

In today's world, the story of Adam and Eve is often considered an archaic vestige of a male-dominated religious cult. Yet, when you read below the surface and are willing to let go of some of your contemporary prejudices, you will find a miraculously condensed guide to creating a solid, exciting, and true spiritual union, one in which the equality of men and women is beyond debate and both are free to simply be themselves as a shared soul. I believe that the secrets to creating a marriage that combines the best of the freedoms of this age with the best of traditional values of the past can be found in just three tiny biblical chapters. That's what I think today's Adams and Eves are looking for and need. I know I was looking for it, desperately needed it, and am glad I found it.

Marriage is the foundation of everything human. It's the cornerstone of families, communities, nations, and all human civilization. A happy, spiritually based marriage between you and your mate is critical not just for your own well-being, but for the well-being of all humanity—as well as all life in the Garden.

Our world *is* the Garden of Eden. Our world is that perfect paradise that God placed here for male and female to enjoy together. The doors to that paradise are never closed, unless your mind is closed.

There is a cherub forever stationed in the east, with a blazing sword of light, leading every Adam and Eve home to a blissful marriage, if they're willing to start out fresh.

Like the original Adam and Eve, allow yourselves to be innocent.

Let yourselves be naked—without shame.

I
A Heavenly Marriage:
You, God, and the Garden

MARRIAGE SECRET #1

There's always a beginning

In the beginning... God created the heavens and the earth.
(Genesis 1:1)

Are you and your Adam or Eve stuck in a rut? The first marital secret of the Garden is not just the foundation of a true spiritual marriage, but also the spiritual foundation of the entire universe. It declares boldly, decisively, even defiantly:

There is no such thing as a rut, because there is such a thing as a beginning.

A *beginning*? It's a very strange idea when you think about it. However, it's also a huge spiritual concept, one upon which every other marriage secret is built.

Seasons come and go, and start all over again. Children are fathered and mothered, then grow into fathers and mothers. The moon goes around and around the earth, while the earth goes around and around the sun. Where is the "beginning"? Which came first, the chicken or the egg? Is there really such a thing as a beginning? A beginning is something we accept casually, but its actual existence is not very obvious.

In the ancient world, no one believed in "beginnings." The world was considered an eternal cycle after cycle. All life, all civilization, the entire cosmos—everything was considered rigidly bound to the cycles of nature. Reality was seen as an eternal roller-coaster ride: up and down, up and down. Human civilizations might be built up, but it was inevitable that they would fall. This was fate. Just look at the number of ancient civilizations that rose and fell; history books are littered with them. In the ancient world, there didn't seem to be any hope or any purpose. Humanity was stuck in a cosmic rut: up and down, rising and falling. All human activity seemed doomed to failure. There was no future. Sadly, you may feel that way about your marriage right now.

But then an inspired band of nomads, the Hebrews, made a historical breakthrough. They introduced the world to a very radical spiritual idea, which we now take for granted: a beginning. They perceived that the cycles of nature didn't just go on and on. They had a beginning, an origin. This origin was the spiritual origin of everything. The true beginning of all beginnings was an eternal, conscious, and ever present Being commonly called "God."

God is the Creator of all the cycles of nature. God is supernatural—not as in a "superstition," but as in *beyond nature*, which is what the word literally means. God is an invisible, formless Being, not bound to any hopeless cycle within the visible world. Indeed, no cycle of nature is a power unto itself; there is only one power, God, who is *the* beginning beyond all beginnings, expressing one power as all things visible or invisible within creation.

This had dramatic consequences for the history of the world, as it does for every Adam and Eve today. After all, if you connect to God, there must always be a beginning. There must always be a way out of a hopeless cycle. There must always be a way to get off the roller-coaster ride.

Perhaps you are on a roller coaster in your marriage right now. It's not uncommon. Many times in marriage, and in all aspects of life, we get stuck on a roller coaster:

> Adam continuously comes home grumpy from work, and Eve continuously dodges his mood and "feeds him quick" to control him. This is a cycle of *fear*.

> Eve may constantly be trying to manipulate a less-than-generous Adam for money, even to the point of withholding sex. This is a cycle of *control* and *anger*.

> Adam may feel more himself around his buddies than around Eve, so Eve feels increasingly lonely. This is a cycle of *self-indulgence* and *despair*.

Eve puts Adam's needs as well as the kids' needs before her own. As a result she feels diminished, exhausted, and creatively useless. This is a cycle of *low self-esteem*.

These are such fairly common cycles that sometimes they are considered just part of a "normal" marriage. However, they are not normal. They are spiritual problems that need to be addressed.

These days, there are also considerably more dangerous cycles: cycles around alcohol or drugs, cycles of abuse, cycles of violence, cycles of marital infidelity, and cycles of marriage after re-marriage.

But, no matter what cycles you're going through, no matter what mistakes you and your mate are currently making in your marriage or your life, the important thing to remember is:

There is hope. There is hope because there is such a thing as a beginning. There is hope because there is such a thing as God.

The cycles you're stuck in don't have to recur. There is a God, a higher power beyond you, and beyond all cycles. In fact, as a general rule, when problems start to cycle and recycle, it's a sign that, like the biblical couple, you've lost your connection to God.

Don't worry. There's always a way back to Eden. No matter what marital problems you've created for yourselves, no matter what spiritual exile you are going through in your marriage, you are not stuck.

You may think you're stuck. But, you're *not* stuck. In fact, you *cannot be* stuck. It's impossible to be stuck, because the universe is simply not designed that way.

There is always a beginning. To believe otherwise is the serpent's deceit. Beware of the serpent.

MARRIAGE SECRET #2

Align yourselves to God's order

And God separated the light from the darkness.
(Genesis 1:4)

Many of today's Adams and Eves think of a marriage as something that takes place in a vacuum, disconnected from the entire universe. They think that the only thing they need to consider in their marriage is their own wants and desires; they need only concern themselves with living in their own private piece of the Garden. However, this is one of the most lethal mistakes any married couple can make.

It may make you angry at first to hear this, but *your marriage is not just your own*. It is not just *your* marriage. Your marriage touches upon family. It touches upon neighbors. It touches upon the trees, the grass, and the alley cat. It touches upon the planet, our solar system, and countless worlds beyond. "Your" marriage is really "our" marriage. It belongs to all of us, since all humanity and all existence are bound by a common relationship forged by God "in the beginning." So, how you conduct your marriage touches upon everything and everyone in creation, as these few examples show:

> When today's Adams and Eves act angrily or cruelly toward each other, they add anger and cruelty to the world. They are spreading their problems into the spiritual atmosphere the whole world breathes. TV shows and movies based upon such cruel marriages amplify the problem. You may not realize it, but this contributes to the atmosphere that creates terrorism in the world.

> When today's Adam and Eve make love, they are not just "doing it." Their bodies are actually God's creation expressing itself through the human sexual act. You may not realize it, but your sex life actually has ecological implications that affect the entire world, as the AIDS crisis has shown.

> When self-indulgent Adams or Eves put their own social life before their children, and ignore them, they are actually contaminating eternity. The problems they create for their children can live on generation after generation, robbing the future before it's begun. The whole world suffers, over and over again, for the mistake of one negligent couple.

The first step to transforming your marriage is to begin to see it with this kind of cosmic perspective, through the eyes of God, so to speak. You must stop looking at your marriage as if it is isolated from existence and begin to appreciate the fact that your marriage actually touches upon infinity. You must begin to comprehend marriage in terms of the enormity it comprehends: an infinite, eternal relationship between you, God, and all creation.

Pause here, and do not read any further until this sinks in. It is at the heart of all the marriage secrets that follow.

There is an order to God's creation. The universe was not just created willy-nilly, but by a supreme intelligence. Just as there are material laws, such as $E = mc^2$, that govern the relationship between energy and matter, there are also spiritual laws that govern the relationship between Adam and Eve. A true spiritual marriage always takes place within this order; it must operate by and cooperate with the laws of creation. This is something that no couple can escape. There is no escaping the spiritual laws of the universe, because there is no other universe, at least that we know of, to which we can move.

Should you attempt to escape God's order, like the biblical couple did, your marriage will fall into "exile" from God. Like the biblical Adam and Eve, you will also experience difficulties, divisiveness, headaches, heartaches, and an assortment of life's little "curses" in your marriage. As unpleasant as these are, they are really God's greatest gifts—little lessons whose purpose is to make you aware of your marital mistake and guide you back on the road to

Eden. We'll talk more about this later on, but, for now, it's best that you simply accept the fact that there is an order to God's Garden and learn about it. The quality of your marriage depends on your learning about the nature of God's order, how God designed it, how it operates, what its purpose is, and—most important—how to conduct your marriage according to it.

There are many aspects to God's order, but the three most fundamental aspects are *freedom, oneness,* and *goodness.*

Certainly, freedom is part of God's order. After all, the order was created by a God who might actually be said to *be* freedom: unrestricted, unlimited, and unbounded. The order of the universe is born of the nature of God who *is* Freedom Itself.

The freedom of God's order is not just something "out there," but is very real, personal, and intimate. It is at the deepest core of our spiritual nature as human beings. As the story of Adam and Eve shows us, God has implanted within each and every male and female a hearty measure of divine freedom. It's commonly called free will, a piece of God's own nature as freedom within us. It is this free will that gives us the ability to align—or un-align—ourselves with God's order, the choice to experience joy in the Garden or banishment.

In any true spiritual marriage, freedom is of cosmic importance, because you are respecting the very presence of God within you and between you. Today's Adam and Eve must respect each other's freedom, not because this is politically correct, democratic, liberated, or a matter of equal rights. They must respect each other's freedom, because freedom is the very nature of God.

For this reason, your need for personal freedom in marriage doesn't ever have to be justified to anyone—not even to your own mate. It doesn't have to be justified to society, to religions, or to any mere mortal institution. It is God, the authority greater than all of them, who has given you freedom. Therefore, to beg to feel free in your marriage is against God, and any marriage that stifles your freedom is not of God.

This notwithstanding, as flesh and blood creatures who are given freedom, but not the unlimited, unrestricted, and unbounded freedom of God—there's a "divine limit" to the degree of your personal freedom in marriage and in the Garden. There is an order to the Garden: God's order (and "order" is another word for "commandment"). There are certain things you cannot do, certain trees you cannot eat of, or even touch. In a marriage aligned to the laws of God's Garden, you cannot simply do what you wish to do when you wish to do it; nor can your mate. The order of which you are a part is considerably larger than your particular ego.

When the biblical Adam and Eve fell, it was because they abused freedom in their marriage; they violated the order of the Garden, God's order. This was because they didn't fully understand the power of their free will and the effect it can have on everyone and everything in the universe. That's why God gave them a swift, painful lesson in responsibility: so they wouldn't inadvertently upset God's Garden even more.

Unfortunately, many of today's Adams and Eves don't consider the effect of their personal freedom on others. They seem to be more concerned with enjoying themselves, making money, building careers, or finding the "perfect" sex life. In essence, they operate according to their own order rather than God's and, as the biblical couple proved, that's a one-way ticket to marital hell.

If we are going to prevent marriages from dissolving and anchor them on a solid spiritual foundation, our God-given freedom must be used responsibly. It must be aligned to God's order. One of the simplest ways to begin doing this is to ask yourself five questions before making any decision or taking any action, either individually or together as a couple:

How does this decision affect each one of us?

How does this decision affect the family?

How does this decision affect our society?

How does this decision affect our world?

How does this decision affect all future generations?

No matter what the decision—even something like the purchase of a car or what food to eat—these questions will help you see your choices in a cosmic context, through the eyes of God. They will help you look beyond yourselves to see that your marriage is part of a greater humanity, of the entire world, and of eternity. They will help stop you from making selfish decisions that could violate yourselves or others, thereby repeating the mistake of the biblical couple.

Most important, these questions will give you time to think. So many of today's Adams and Eves operate according to "sound-byte" attention spans. They are moving so fast, trying to squeeze it all in, that they don't slow down and realize what they are actually sowing and reaping in the Garden. They don't stop to reflect on the value system they are using to make their decisions and shape their lives. Asking these questions will give you an opportunity to weigh your decision, to make sure that you consider all these different aspects of God's order.

After all, besides freedom, oneness is also a fundamental aspect of God's order. The entire universe was born of oneness, which is the supreme quality of the Creator. Everything in creation is intricately wedded to everything else in a single cosmic "marriage" forged in oneness by God's oneness. So, to further align your marriage to God's order, it is absolutely critical that you never intentionally violate a sense of oneness, unity, harmony, or peace between you both, or you will be literally shredding the fabric of reality. This was the biblical couple's mistake, and there's no faster way to marital exile.

Having free will means you can create your own heaven or your own hell by your choices. So, you must always choose to bring the oneness of God into everything you do. You must choose to create oneness not just between you, but between everyone and everything with which you come into contact. Your boss, your mother-in-law, and the grocery clerk are all part of your marriage, because they are all part of the oneness of existence. All people and all life in the Garden must share in the oneness of the marriage you create or it will not be a true spiritual marriage. The more oneness you sow through your marriage, the more oneness you will reap, and therefore the more stable, loving, and "two-as-one" your marriage will be.

Remember, the opposite of oneness is divisiveness, duality, and destruction. That's the serpent's path. Don't go down it. Resist temptation!

Last, and perhaps most important, God's order reflects another sublime aspect of God's nature: goodness. Goodness is so much a part of the nature of God that the word "God" is actually a contraction of the word "good"; God could be said to be "concentrated good."

Good, good, good, good, good, good. Six times in Genesis, God declares the world to be "good," and the seventh time, as if to top it off, God declares the world to be "very good." Just look at the sky, the trees, the smell of a newborn infant. Is there any doubt about God's intention being good? Is there any doubt that this Garden was born of God's goodness, before human beings fell and upset the balance?

So, in a true spiritual marriage, you must always use your free will to choose what is good, or you will un-align yourselves to the order of the Garden, disconnecting your marriage from the essential goodness of God.

Good means kindness. Good means compassion. Good means honesty. Good means treating each other as you would like to be treated. Good means not doing anything that is harmful, whether in thought, word, or deed. Last, but certainly not least, good also means love. Bringing God's supreme nature as love into your marriage is as good as it gets.

The good in your marriage is supposed to be created naturally. If you are going around with a "painted face," creating a facade of goodness in order to appear to be doing what's right in order to impress somebody, that's not really good. God's goodness expresses itself as natural goodness, free flowing and joyful. In a spiritual marriage, the goal is to naturally express your goodness, innocently, like the newly created Adam and Eve. If you are always trying to be good, and not doing so straight from the heart, that effort is often a form of control and manipulation disguised as goodness. Be very careful. The serpent's deceit can even masquerade as God.

Together, freedom, oneness, and goodness weave the fabric of God's order. Lack of any one will throw the order of the Garden off balance and lead to a fall. Freedom without oneness can be chaos. Oneness without freedom can be a prison. Goodness without oneness can be self-indulgence. Oneness without goodness can be servitude. Goodness without freedom can be naiveté. Freedom without goodness is dangerous.

If you wish to have a true spiritual marriage, you must align yourselves to all three of these divine qualities, and seek to balance them in your lives. The more you do, the easier and more joyful your marriage will become. Your marriage will no longer be going against the entire flow of the universe, but instead will be flowing along with it. Aligned to God's intention, you will no longer need to pump all sorts of effort and work into your marriage to keep it going. The more each of you concentrates your spiritual energy on aligning yourselves, individually and together, to God's order, the more the entire force of creation will automatically propel your marriage forward. Your marriage will grow in freedom, oneness, and goodness, as does everything else in existence.

This is the experience of what is traditionally called "grace," "providence," "divine love," "God's protection," "living-in-Spirit," or "God's guidance," depending on which spiritual tradition you follow. It's the stuff of which a marriage made in heaven is made.

MARRIAGE SECRET #3

Be totally dependent on each other

Then the man said,
"This at last is bone of my bones
and flesh of my flesh."
(Genesis 2:23)

In today's highly individualistic world, there is one issue that is extremely difficult, if not outright threatening, for Adam and Eve to deal with: dependency. In my opinion, not dealing with dependency is the single biggest cause of breakups in marriages and families.

Especially since the feminist revolution, the mere thought of dependency has been enough to make Eve and Adam bristle. A feeling of dependency can make Eve feel "weaker" in relationship to Adam; it can make her feel like she's not her own person ("I'm my mother"), that she's not standing on her own two feet as women are supposed to do in today's era. A feeling of dependency can also disturb Adam deep down to his masculine core; he can feel enslaved to Eve's whims, "castrated" by her, plagued by a constant ache to bolt from the marriage.

Dependency brings to the surface all sorts of mother and father complexes, all sorts of issues around being treated like a child. It's a psychological stick of dynamite, ready to explode. Dependency can create resentment, which is anger held inside. It doesn't take long for the anger to erupt: "You're smothering me!" "Get off my butt!" Such anger, however, is usually just an emotional cover-up for the deep fear of dependency that we all have within us.

The fear of dependency is built into us from the moment we are born. It's a bodily fear built into our "animal skins" for survival. A newborn who is not physically supported by his or her parent will splay its arms with fear of falling. Similarly, when the "newborn" Adam and Eve lost the support of their Divine Parent, they too felt the fear of falling.

From a spiritual vantage point, however, dependency is nothing to fear. On the contrary, dependency is something that should be embraced, loved, and relished. Dependency should never be avoided in a healthy spiritual marriage. In fact, dependency can never be avoided. Why? Because dependency is part of God's design for the universe, and Adam and Eve can't run away from the universe or from God.

We see dependency fearfully only when we look at it through the lens of our own childlike vulnerability. However, when we look at dependency through the lens of adult spiritual strength, we can see something else. To experience dependency is actually to experience God's Love in disguise. Just think about all the loving dependencies God has placed here for us:

> Adam and Eve would not be able to eat if creation did not include food.

> Adam and Eve would not be able to breathe if creation did not include air.

> Adam and Eve would not be able to procreate if their secretions did not contain water from oceans.

> The carbon, hydrogen, nitrogen, and oxygen of Adam and Eve's bodies are elemental "ribs" they exchange in total dependency with each other, all life, and the entire universe.

The fact is that we are all totally dependent by nature. We are totally dependent upon everything in existence. You couldn't escape dependency if you tried. So, to view dependency as a problem or something to be feared—as today's Adam and Eve often do—is actually to deny God and God's order. It is a ticket to exile. Moreover, to blame your mate for your dependency is a spiritual lie. It is not your mate who makes you dependent; it is God who makes you dependent.

Total dependency is the nature of God's order, and a true spiritual marriage, aligned to that order, must be one of total dependency. Such a marriage accepts total dependency, honors it, and even seeks to intensify it, because it is God's will for everything in existence, including marriages.

In a totally dependent marriage, Adam feels absolute freedom to be totally dependent upon Eve, and Eve feels absolute freedom to be totally dependent upon Adam. Both feel totally and joyfully free to make demands on the other, knowing these are not really "demands." Both give and receive of themselves freely, like everything in creation, with complete and generous abandon. Both act toward the other with the knowledge that they are both totally dependent parts of the universe. God didn't scrimp on creation, so neither do the two partners in a totally dependent relationship scrimp on each other.

For example, regarding two of the most "touchy" dependency issues in a marriage, money and sex:

> In a totally dependent marriage, Adam and Eve realize that their money is not theirs, even if they earned it. Instead, money is viewed like everything in creation, as a gift of God. They do not withhold it from the other to control the other, but give of it freely and generously, as God would, with no ulterior motive except sharing God's love.

> In a totally dependent marriage, Adam and Eve are totally dependent sexually upon each other's bodies.

Their bodies are joyfully available to each other, without headaches or prodding. There is no sexual manipulation, just totally dependent intimacy, the sharing of God's creation in the form of their physical bodies.

When you are living according to the law of total dependency, you begin to see yourself as a channel, avenue, or vehicle by which God gives to the universe through you. In your marriage, you make yourself open to being a conduit for God's own desire to give to the other through you. You allow God to work through you *as* you.

To do otherwise is to actually block the flow of God's goodness to each other and the world of which you are a totally dependent part. This is exactly what happens to many marriages in which one or the other partner becomes too powerful or egotistical or attempts to control or limit the other. This kind of behavior can prevent God's blessings from entering your marriage; it can actually stifle the flow of creation's abundance into your lives, bringing pain and suffering to both of you, as it did to the biblical Adam and Eve. Like them, you will have actually chosen to block God's protection, as the serpent looks on, laughing.

In the biblical story, Adam and Eve were so newly created that they didn't know the law of total dependency. Adam was so locked inside his head that he was completely unaware of Eve's needs or feelings. Eve, newly "separated" from Adam, followed her own frivolous desires, not thinking about the effect of her actions on Adam or on God's order. In a Garden built upon the law of total dependency, breaking that law brought punitive consequences. Adam became dominant; he would now be overly attentive to what Eve was doing, becoming enslaved by that dominance to labor and support her. Eve became submissive; she would now be overly solicitous of Adam, becoming dependent upon him as the channel for her support. The restrictive roles of the past were essentially a hard, mutual lesson in the law of total dependency.

Yet, despite their greater sophistication, education, and liberation, today's Adams and Eves have not mastered total dependency any better. In today's "me-generation," Adam and Eve have often become so self-centered, so excessively free as individuals, that they cannot form a lasting marriage. Making matters worse, out of rebellious anger they've thrown off all the roles of the past, so now they have nothing to hold them together. Breaking the law of total dependency has produced a bumper crop of human-made punishments in today's Garden: divorce, serial monogamy, cohabitation, prenuptial agreements, palimony, broken families, single mothers, absentee fathers, latchkey kids—a whole series of makeshift band-aids that cover up the spiritual wound, but never heal it.

We all need to wake up from our deep sleep. Only a totally-dependent marriage—where each of you is individually dependent upon God and creation, and both of you are mutually dependent upon each other—can solve the egalitarian marriage problems of today. Every other solution is just superficial. It doesn't get to the core. The core is total dependency, the absolute, spiritual inescapability of total dependency in your marriage and in the universe.

In this, God gives you no choice: you either work to create total dependency between you, willingly learning to cooperate with this law of the Garden, or your marriage will be fighting the universe, an uphill battle doomed to failure.

> Are you ready to be totally dependent on your mate without fear of being controlled, dominated, or infantilized?
>
> Are you ready to be totally dependent on your mate without asserting your ego, taking advantage, or hemming your mate in?
>
> Are you brave enough to risk feeling vulnerable to your mate, without fear of going backwards to the abusive roles of the past?

It's not easy to break down your emotional defenses and remove the "fig leaves" that separate you as mates. But one thing I can assure you, from personal experience: if you practice the law of total dependency and keep practicing it until it ceases to be a rigid law and becomes a loving art between you, the doors to Eden will fly open.

Through total dependency, your marriage will find new life in God's Garden.

MARRIAGE SECRET #4

Always remember, you are dust

Then the LORD God formed man from the dust of the ground.
(Genesis 2:7)

There is one four-letter word that can change your marriage forever. It is not the usual one you use when arguments have gone too far. It's a four-letter word that can prevent any and all arguments, if you keep it in mind: dust.

Dust—that lifeless, disrespectful stuff that accumulates on furniture—is a major ingredient in the recipe for a heavenly marriage. Indeed, next to an abundant supply of love, nothing is more critical than an ample sprinkling of dust.

Simply put, dust means humility; it is from dust that we are born and to dust that we return. Dust means knowing your place in God's scheme of things. Dust means knowing you are mortal and behaving that way, never disregarding others or undermining the order of creation, as the biblical couple did. Dust means being constantly aware that you are not the sole purpose of existence and that your particular ego is not judge and jury of all humanity. You are certainly a magnificent creation of God; however, even as such, you are just one infinitesimally small particle of dust in the cosmos.

Perhaps you've seen one of those "traditional" marriages, where Adam seems to be a know-it-all, often about finances or business, and Eve is disregarded as a mindless female. Or perhaps you've witnessed a marriage where Eve contemptuously brushes Adam off, as if he is just a silly boy who needs to have his butt wiped. This is a classic example of a "dustless" marriage, a marriage where there is no humility, a marriage where one partner or the other has set himself or herself up as the authority, the expert, the ruler, or the lord over the other.

Unfortunately, in today's era, dust remains a scarce commodity, with a lethal effect upon marriage and family life. In today's Garden, the pursuit of power, money, and personal gratification is so all-encompassing that dust doesn't settle and marriages aren't stable. In today's Garden, the dominant message is not humility, but rather lack of humility. The media exalts the ego, intensifies lust for personal power, and feeds both male and female dreams of wealth, power, and control over others. Add to this a considerable competition between the sexes and you have a marriage with no solid ground for a couple to stand on, no dust beneath their feet.

However, with an adequate sprinkling of dust, today's marriages can take on a whole new life:

In a dust-inspired marriage, men do not claim power. Women do not claim power. Men do not defer to women. Women do not defer to men. Neither one wrestles to "wear the pants."

In a dust-inspired marriage, both partners refuse absolute power over the other. They don't refuse it because they are weak, or frail, or submissive, or because they are "less of a man" or "less liberated." They refuse it because they consider God the only absolute power.

In a dust-inspired marriage, even if you choose separate or "traditional roles," one role is never considered better than the other. The breadwinner and the cook and bottle washer are both dust, humbly doing their jobs for the mutual benefit of both.

In a dust-inspired marriage, today's Adam and Eve humbly enjoy certain equality as men and women; they are both equally dust. Indeed, knowing you are dust can create a lot of freedom for both of you:

When you know you are dust, you are less apt to take charge. This can free you up from a lot of guilt. After all, the greater the burden you take on, the more blame falls to you when something goes wrong.

When you can accept that you are dust, you don't have to work as hard in order to prove you're worthy of being loved. You don't have to be one of those perfect wives or perfect husbands who exhaust themselves as do-gooders, only to end up feeling angry, betrayed, and exhausted.

When you know you are dust, you never overstep your bounds. You're more willing to allow God to handle the excess caretaking. You respect your limitations as a human being, giving without exhausting yourself, sharing without taking on more than your share of troubles, helping without fixing others.

Knowing you are dust doesn't just open your marriage to more freedom. It also opens your marriage to divine wisdom:

When you know you are dust, you can admit you don't know everything. That's the beginning of all wisdom.

When you know you are dust, you are open to seeking God's guidance, forming a relationship with a mind that is greater than yours.

When you know you are dust, you are more receptive to the intelligence that created the order of the Garden, so your marriage is more open to God's grace. This can stop you from creating serious problems, which may be painful to undo later on.

In a healthy spiritual marriage, you need to continuously —over and over again—remind yourselves that you are dust. Should one of you forget that you are dust, the other has a spiritual obligation to remind and lovingly say to the other:

"Darling, I hear what you are saying. But, I'm not so certain I agree with you. After all, you are just dust now, aren't you? And I know I'm dust, too. So let's put our egos in the dustbin."

A simple, shared reminder that you are dust can be humorously offered, with a wink and an endearing, even sexy, smile. Such a reminder should be sufficient to defuse any argument before it begins, because it punctures the haughtiness of ego that is always lying underneath any argument. Such a reminder should also be sufficient to permit any partner in the marriage the right to be heard, the right to be considered, and the right to present a different or contrary view.

But one word of warning, lest the serpent lure you away: true humility is not, as unfortunately has been taught by some fallen religions, *humiliation*. Humility does not mean degrading yourself or your mate. Humility does not mean embarrassing each other, enfeebling the other, putting your partner down in private or public, or forcing the other to be humble. Nor is humility that fake passivity or phony niceness that so many pious people display. Under such facades are often "wolves in sheep's clothing," drooling for prey.

Developing true humility does not require you to lower yourself, hide yourself, or debase yourself. It does not mean you must become overly self-conscious or even hyper-vigilant as to whether you are doing something right or wrong. Developing true humility doesn't mean you must constantly have your eyes focused down on the ground.

Quite the contrary. To develop true humility is a joyful, spiritually elevating task. It's as simple as looking up on a starlit night to the source of all existence. It's as simple as taking in, with breathless wonder, the enormity of God's creation, while appreciating simultaneously how tiny you are by comparison.

Take your shoes off. Feel the dust under your feet. Wiggle your toes a bit. Relish the dust you are. No other marriage secret in the Garden is so simple, so sweet, or so immensely powerful.

You may sweep the dust out of your house, but don't be too meticulous. In a spiritual marriage, always leave a little dust in your hearts. Stay humble.

II
BECOMING SPIRITUAL PARTNERS

MARRIAGE SECRET #5

You're created in God's image

Let us make humankind in our image,
according to our likeness.
(Genesis 1:26)

In today's Garden there's a lot of confusion about what makes a natural man and a natural woman. Is a natural Adam someone who goes out to work every day and never washes a plate? Is a natural Eve someone who bakes cookies and always has a smile on her face? Is a natural Adam some pumped-up macho-type, prone to heroic violence? Is a natural Eve some sleek, long-legged starlet who slays men with a look? Are Eves who are more aggressive and more successful in business more masculine and, therefore, unnatural? Are Adams who are more sensitive and domestically gifted more effeminate and, therefore, unnatural?

In today's gender-bending culture, the images of what makes a natural man and a natural woman are more confusing than ever. The confusion is compounded by Hollywood and the media, which indoctrinate us with biased images of what a true man or a true woman is. Whether we realize it or not, we are continuously being subconsciously imprinted with these images; they are part of a mainstream hypnosis, which we call popular culture. We take these images into our minds. We permit our own self-image to be shaped by them. Consequently, they enter our marriage, influencing our relationship with our spouse. We often judge each other by these images, learning to love or hate ourselves and each other depending on whether we fit these stereotypical images of male and female.

However, from the Bible's perspective, all these images are false. They are not our true image at all. No matter what a man or woman appears like on the outside, that's just a superficial show-of-form. The true image of a natural man and a natural woman is far more glorious, powerful, radiant, and spectacular than we can imagine.

The true image of who we are, both male and female, is God! God is the true standard, the real standard, and the only reliable, unchanging and eternal image for what a natural man and woman are. In fact, men and women are *not natural*, which is why figuring out what's natural is virtually impossible. Like God, in whose image and likeness we are created, we are *super-natural*—beyond nature, as the word literally means. Adam and Eve are two super-natural beings, born of the one Supernatural Being. We are the living, fleshly expression of the God who is beyond nature, and therefore its Creator.

Now this is a considerably more exalted image of men and women than the one with which we are popularly bombarded. Bring this image into your marriage and you can transform your relationship instantly. Think about it:

When was the last time you looked at your mate watching TV, maybe with a beer in his hand, and thought to yourself, "He is made in the image and likeness of God"?

When was the last time you sat across the dinner table and didn't stare down into your plate, but into the eyes of someone reflecting the image and likeness of God?

When was the last time you pressed warmly against your mate, knowing she is made in the image and likeness of God—and not just a body there for your amusement?

What a difference a divine image can make in a marriage. When you begin to relate as males and females according to your super-natural image, you move past the popular illusions and begin to pay attention to what is essential, spiritual, eternal, and even holy about your mate. Hanging bellies, thinning hair, or sagging breasts no longer become your standard for your mate. Your perspective changes from carnal to spiritual: you cease to see your mate as just an object whose sole purpose is to attract you or satisfy you.

When you begin to see your mate as the image and likeness of God, your marriage, no matter how exiled, will instantly realign to God's order. After all, how can you disregard the image and likeness of God? Can you really justify impoliteness or cruelty to the image and likeness of God? Is it possible to not find something beautiful or handsome in the image and likeness of God—regardless of what someone actually looks like? How could anyone, in good conscience, cheat on the image and likeness of God?

In fact, devotion, respect, kindness, caring, consideration, adoration, honesty, nurturing, chivalry, trustworthiness, truthfulness—a list as infinite as the Infinite One—are the only ways to treat the image and likeness of God.

When you correctly view your mate—not according to the warped, twisted, politically correct, fly-by-night, and faddish standards of a fallen-world—but as God created that person to be, you set your spouse free from the serpent's hypnosis. You also set your marriage on the high road. There it will stay—divinely supported in God's Garden—as long as you keep the image of God *as your mate* foremost in your mind and heart.

But let's not forget: you are made in the image and likeness of God too.

Seeing yourself correctly can change how you feel about yourself, and that can also dramatically improve your relationship with your spouse.

Once you look below the surface, so many problems that are considered marital problems are really not. They are psychological and spiritual problems that Adam or Eve have with themselves. These are acted out by one spouse on another, making them into marital problems when they are really personal problems. For example, you may have self-esteem problems that make you feel ugly to your mate or unworthy of love. Sometimes such self-esteem problems can be so bad that you will actually permit your mate to abuse you—either verbally or physically—and consider the abuse justifiable. This is very common in long-term abusive relationships.

However, such problems begin to disappear the moment you begin to see yourself as you truly are: the image and likeness of God. Even long-term abuse problems can begin to dissolve the moment you claim your super-natural right to divine respect:

When you realize you're made in the image and likeness of God, you love yourself more. That makes you more loving to your mate.

When you realize you're made in the image and likeness of God, you feel more beautiful, regardless of your looks. You radiate a self-esteem that's based upon spiritual essence, not superficial appearance.

When you realize you're made in the image and likeness of God, you expect more out of life, and

so you receive more out of life. Certainly second-
best could never be good enough for God's own
image.

To be created in the image and likeness of God means
that each of you carries within you the spark of God's very
own being. The word for "image" in the original Hebrew
of the Bible, *tzelem*, actually means to be cut off. You are
actually cut off or parceled out of the one Spirit from
whom the entire universe was born. You are a living indi-
vidualization of God's holy essence, so you yourself possess
God's qualities: freedom, oneness, and goodness—scaled
down to human existence.

Being created in the image and likeness of God means
you also have another quality that you inherit from your
Divine Parent: creativity. Indeed, creativity is the spiritual
hallmark of being made in God's image and likeness.

Within every Adam and Eve is a creative dynamo, the
Creator's own power. You are creators born of the Creator.
As creative beings, you have the astonishing power to sow
and reap your desires in God's Garden. You can decide
what you'd like to accomplish and accomplish it. You can
plant the seeds of your imagination through your thoughts,
words, ideas, and actions—and reap a harvest of exciting
experiences. As creative beings with free will, you can also
sow and reap failure, or sow and reap success. You can sow
and reap evil or overwhelming goodness.

Just as God spoke a word and set creation in motion,
you too can speak a word—utter an inspired thought—and

let your creativity fly into motion. The greatest human achievements—all our technologies, enterprises, art, music, literature (including the Bible), and all our dreams—are created by Adam and Eve simply being like God, being creative like the Creator. Indeed, everything you will ever achieve in your life personally, or together as a married couple, is achieved through the exact same divine talent.

Adam was not intended by God to just labor in the fields, plucking thorns hopelessly, nor was Eve intended to be restricted just to physical creativity, in pain. Your creativity was not intended by God to be used just for labor. That's why marriages in which partners don't express their divine creativity can experience tremendous pressure. One or the other can feel unsatisfied. They can feel they are missing something from life: "I am not what I could have been." They may actually blame the other for holding them back. Such a situation is often marked by tension. This can lead to anger, which, when held back, can lead to self-hatred or depression: "I feel all closed in."

It is simply not natural for males and females to not utilize their super-natural gift of creativity. Denying your creativity will stifle the image and likeness of God from being expressed through your marriage. You will be hiding your light under a bushel, holding back the spiritual power that is the foundation of a heavenly relationship between mates.

However, when Adam and Eve are both creative individuals, dynamically expressing God-within-them, this adds a powerful lift to marriage. God's own energy enters the relationship. Each spouse becomes more exciting to the other. Couples who express their creativity are generally happier, because they are doing what they love to do. They are generally more successful monetarily, because they will joyfully work harder and so they will accomplish more. Temperaments improve because no one comes home quite as exhausted or grumpy.

Most important, when you are thinking creatively, you are thinking with a higher mind, the mind of the Creator in you. That's why creativity is one of the fastest ways to open the door to the experience of God's grace. Creativity forms an instantaneous super-natural connection to the Supernatural Creator. You become a vehicle by which God continues the work of creation through your thoughts, words, and hands. It's fun to be creative. You don't even have to work to establish your connection to God. It happens in a simple, childlike fashion—spontaneously, innocently, and joyfully, as if you were freshly fashioned children of God, like the biblical couple.

When you're in this kind of creative mode, you become, in essence, a co-creator with God. The image and likeness you are becomes a conduit through which God's freedom, oneness, and goodness are amplified by your thoughts, words, and actions to expand the goodness in the Garden even more than God could do alone. To amplify God's goodness in and through your marriage is the purpose of your divine creativity as a couple.

In summary, I offer this creative exercise to every Adam and Eve brave enough to try it:

You and your mate take off your clothes. Stand together, holding hands, in front of a full-length mirror. Now, take a good, long, detailed look at your naked selves as a couple:

What's the image you see?

Do you like what you see?

> Do you see things that are wrong, or things that are wonderful? Do you pay more attention to what you see as a "defect" than to what you see as "correct"?

> Do you see two images of God standing there, or two images of the serpent?

Now, spend a little time every day consciously working on changing the image you have of your mate and of yourself. Share your thoughts with each other. Don't be ashamed. You're only human. We all make unfair judgments.

Don't stop until all you see in the mirror are two images and likenesses of God. In a very short amount of time, you'll notice a dramatic improvement in the quality of your marriage.

The image you have of each other is the marriage you'll have between you. It's that simple.

MARRIAGE SECRET #6

Be spiritual equals

And the rib that the LORD God had taken from the man
he made into a woman.
(Genesis 2:22)

These days, the story of Adam and Eve is often badly maligned. It is touted as being a male-dominated, patriarchal myth designed to reduce women to a subordinate state, to demean them and to justify male dominance in marriage and in society. It is considered a sexist story to be shunned.

However, contrary to such popular thinking, the story of Adam and Eve does not teach this nor is it intended to institutionalize such cruelty in marriage. Its major message to both men and women is this: you are spiritual equals.

But before we discuss this critical marriage message, let's swiftly and decisively de-bunk all the nonsense about this tale being sexist.

According to many Bible translations, the first chapter of Genesis says, "God created MAN in HIS own image, in the image of God HE created HIM" (Gen 1:27). This is followed immediately with "male and female, HE created THEM" (emphases added). This may seem sexist, with God being referred to as a "he" and Adam being created in God's "male image," that is, as a "him." However, the word "man" in the original Hebrew, *Adam*, means humankind or humanity, both male and female. You could say that Eve is a "female Adam" and Adam is a "male Adam." The word "he" or "him" is neuter in Hebrew, and can also mean "it." Therefore, God is neither male nor female and the first "man" is neither male nor female. God's image and likeness refers to both man and woman.

In fact, the original man, according to some early interpretations, was considered a hermaphrodite, having both sexual natures. The word "rib" in Hebrew can also mean a "side." So you could say that the original Adam, a hermaphrodite, forfeited a side or aspect of "himself" to create Eve. Eve expressed the power to bear life. Adam, with his female side now living outside him, became a "normal male," expressing the power to spark life. Indeed, before Eve was created, there actually was no "real male," only a dual-sexed human, representing all humanity.

All of this explains the mysterious pluralized God in the first chapter of Genesis: "Let US make humankind in OUR image, according to OUR likeness" (Gen 1:26, emphasis added). It's there to make sure no one could possibly think that God's image didn't include both male and female. The Hebrew word for "God" in the first chapter of Genesis is *Elohim*, a plural word that literally means "gods" and originally referred to the multiple gods, male gods and female goddesses, that were worshiped prior to the time of the Hebrews. After the rise of belief in one God, these gods and goddesses became thought of as sides or aspects of the one God, just as Adam and Eve were sides or aspects of God's one image. In time, the word *Elohim* came to be used as a singular name for God, especially when God acts specifically as the Creator. This makes perfect sense, since creation is composed of both male and female forces, "gods," which weave in and through nature.

Moreover, in the second chapter of Genesis, the Hebrew name used for God is YHVH-Elohim, which is often poorly translated "Lord God." YHVH is the present tense of the Hebrew word "to be" and could be translated "being," which is neither male nor female—just pure creative-essence itself. So, you could say the double name of God used in the second chapter of Genesis could be translated: "Creative Being with both male and female aspects as one Creator God." There's no sexism here.

Finally, as the coup de grace to the Bible's supposed sexism: in the story, it is actually Eve who is stronger, more domineering, self-interested, worldly, power-lusting, and sexual. It is Eve who discovers her free will first. Adam seems just a passive male—quite dumb and oblivious—

totally lacking Eve's intelligence, resourcefulness, spunkiness, and willfulness. Obviously, the Bible was well aware of the power of women and the relative weakness of men. Modern biologists, if not staunch feminists, will tell you the same thing.

So let there be no doubt about it. If anyone tries to use the Bible to justify a system in which men have a divine right to dominate women and women must submit, don't be lured. The serpent can appear in many guises, including the robes of clergy. The Bible teaches that all men and women are spiritual equals. This is how God designed them to be. As in the story, it is only when Adam and Eve lose their connection to God that they fall into crude dominant and submissive behavior. Conversely, if you see any of today's Adams and Eves locked into this kind of behavior, it is pretty certain they've lost their connection to God.

Spiritual equality is therefore the only way to conduct a marriage that's aligned to God's order. To be spiritual equals means that the great spiritual gifts that come with being created in God's image and likeness are to be as equally expressed by today's Eve as by today's Adam. Both are entitled to express their individual free will, seek oneness, and explore their personal good, because both were made in the image of the freedom, oneness, and goodness of God. And, of course, with regard to creativity (the hallmark of our super-natural natures), that's something both women and men are equally entitled to express, sowing their talents and reaping their rewards to the delight of creation and God, with no bias from serpent-influenced preju-

dices. After all, both Adam and Eve are equally co-creators
born of the Creator.

Spiritual equality means that both Adam and Eve must
be unabashedly free to allow their spirits to soar, because
their spirits are God's. This is not up for debate. This is not
something to be negotiated in any marriage. No chauvinist
need deny it. No feminist need support it. There are no
two ways about it. Spiritual equality is part of the unwritten
laws of the universe, built into every marriage contract,
whether it's expressly spelled out there or not.

Married couples, especially long-term married couples,
often forget this. They unconsciously tug at the other person's spirit, plying, bending, controlling, directing. Many an
Adam has been worn down in marriage because he has mar-
tyred himself to support a woman's extravagances. Many an
Eve has been put down in marriage, unable to release the
God-given talents within her because she's too busy tending
to the desires of her husband. But no human spirit can be
owned by another human being, even by a mate. That's not
marriage. That's enslavement, and that's what feminism jus-
tifiably rebelled against, for enslavement of women is what
the institution of marriage had become.

Your spirit is owned only by God. By virtue of the light
God has placed in you, your marriage must never, ever be
permitted to dwarf your own personal fulfillment. You are
not together for the purpose of sacrificing yourselves into
extinction to keep the marriage together. Such a marriage
is hardly worth keeping together; it is a violation of God
and God's order.

This said, however, be careful. The serpent has prepared a trap, and many of today's Adams and Eves, bombarded with all sorts of bizarre politically correct propaganda, have fallen right into it. Being spiritual equals does not mean that husbands and wives must achieve the exact same degree of success and reward. Being spiritual equals doesn't mean that you should employ a yardstick to measure whether or not you and your mate have an equal spiritual relationship. No wife should feel guilty if she, unlike her more contemporary peers, decides not to pursue a career except childrearing. No man should be embarrassed or made to feel less of a man if his wife happens to garner more money and power. Unfortunately, in today's sexually competitive environment, spiritual equality has turned into different kinds of dominance/submission roles, as equally fallen as the ones in the past.

Sadly, in today's Garden, the word "equality" has been twisted, mangled, and turned upside-down. Equality is often construed to mean that Adam and Eve should be the same or identical. This kind of thinking has spilled over into marriages and has seriously undermined them.

Spiritual equals though you are, men and women are not, and never will be, the same. Eve has different physical abilities, different thresholds for pain, different reactions to stress, different natural rhythms. Her body requires different degrees of attention, especially with regard to reproduction, where Eve does virtually all the work and Adam gets off light. Adam is also very different from Eve, as any woman will quickly tell you—probably with a chuckle—about the male mind.

In today's era, in the name of equality, women have often pushed themselves to be identical to men. They have sometimes imitated men in the workplace in order to appear powerful and get on the fast track. The false standards of men that many of today's Eves have mimicked are largely responsible for the tremendous psychological and physical stress on today's super-women. They are false standards for men. They are even falser standards for women.

Many of today's Adams who have tried to connect to their more sensitive sides to balance the new Eve have also paid the price. Their powerfully exciting "male-magnetism" has often become submerged and stultified. Not a few of today's women's magazines query: "What ever happened to real men?" Psychological difficulties, including impotence, are becoming more prevalent as men try to balance out more liberated females, losing their own fiery maleness in the process. Indeed, today's Adam is often subjected to "male-bashing," his maleness being considered a primitive behavior to be scorned.

God did not create Adam and Eve to be the same. In fact, God did not create anything in all of creation to be the same. There is not one thing, not one plant, not one animal, not one atom of anything that is exactly the same as anything else. God created everything but sameness. The very idea of sameness is an invention of confused, serpent-guided minds.

Here are a few easy tips to help you enhance the spiritual equality in your marriage without falling into the serpent's trap of sameness.

Allow yourselves to enjoy being male and female.

Give each other complete permission to indulge your natural male and female tendencies. Don't force each other to fit any preconceived mold. Don't analyze your behaviors or make one another feel self-conscious about how you naturally are as male or female. Accept each other as you are. Enjoy yourselves as you are. Only then will you notice a natural choreography. You'll begin to see that you are not so much opposites as complements, like heaven and earth.

Allow yourselves to relish some traditional niceties and even practice them together.

There are many traditional behaviors—like opening a car door for a woman, or babying your husband—that, in the extremes of this era, we've repressed. Try practicing some of these niceties between you. Tell your mate what you might like done for you and vice-versa. It will make you both feel special as men and women and safe in your differences as males and females. You might actually find it fun.

Separate responsibilities should be equally valued.

Yes, running a vacuum is as important as earning a living. These tasks should be seen through spiritual eyes as valuable services lovingly rendered—spiritual gifts to a shared home. Never attach a dollar value to such tasks.

There are many household responsibilities that have to be divvied up, especially if today's Adam and Eve have a family. But do not take into your marriage the value system of a fallen world that puts money before everything else so that you end up disparaging the less economic partner and worshiping the more economic one. Remember, it's a general rule of a spiritual household that if you seek what is good, the money will follow.

Allow for plenty of variation and flexibility in your roles.

All Adams and Eves are not necessarily alike. Some women are more male in certain ways than their husbands; some men are more female in certain ways than their wives. As long as there is no ridicule, as long as neither one puts the other down, or takes away the other's self-respect, or violates the principle of total dependency, this should be delighted in. Creation is filled with variation. There is no standard male or standard female. Adjust your marriage to who you are, not to models invented by serpentine minds. Experiment to find what works for both of you in your marriage. Loosen up and be free enough to play with different options.

Respect your body's limits.

The bodies that God created for you are not the same. There are limits that are unique to your male or female constitutions. These should be honored without question.

Men should never push themselves beyond themselves in order to fulfill the expectations of what they think a woman thinks a man should be. Many a heart attack has taken place because Adam was trying to win the approval of an Eve. Nor should Eve ever push herself beyond her physical limits to feel more equal or liberated. This becomes more critical—even life preserving—should Eve decide to have a baby. Remember, the health in those beautiful male and female bodies that God gave you is more important than material expectations from each other or the world's fallen ideas of liberation.

If you honor your spiritual equality, but protect yourselves from the serpent's trap of sameness, you will have discovered one of the most important secrets and mastered one of the most difficult marital lessons of the Garden. You'll not only succeed in being yourselves as men and women, but you'll also succeed in remaining yourselves as males and females in a gender-bending era.

Then you'll be able to forget all this contentious nonsense between the sexes and just get back to basics: the warm, glowing, enticing, intoxicating, and definitely sexy dance of differences between you. That's the way God designed the Garden to be.

Vive la difference. Live your differences.

MARRIAGE SECRET #7

Live like a shared soul

*So the LORD God caused a deep sleep to fall upon the man,
and he slept; then he took one of his ribs
and closed up its place with flesh.
(Genesis 2:21)*

After God's punishment of the biblical couple, a very curious role reversal takes place. Eve, who has been the more dominant and more active partner, now becomes the more submissive and passive partner; Adam, who has been the more submissive and more passive partner, now becomes the more dominant and active partner. Each becomes a mirror to the other.

How could they be otherwise? After all, both are created from the original Adam, a single original human soul. Both share a rib or side of each other. Both are a shared soul—two sides mirroring off each other. Although they possess their own individual connection to God and are spiritually equal, they can fully know themselves only by reflecting in the mirror of their partner. Each is only one-half of a single human soul. Each partner has been spiritually designed by God to have the exact missing piece of the other.

This is the Bible's way of describing the spiritual nature of marriage. You are both two souls interlocked as one. You are both mirrors reflecting aspects of a single human being. So, to have a marriage aligned to God and creation, you must also be aligned to each other. Your shared-soul nature requires you both, male and female, to reflect off of each other and thereby learn from each other. In fact, aside from companionship and reproduction, that's the single most important spiritual purpose behind marriage: to learn from each other.

Because you are a shared soul, by learning about your mate you also can learn a tremendous amount about yourself. Your mate becomes a powerful force to propel your own spiritual advancement:

Do you get angry when your Adam or Eve doesn't replace the roll of toilet paper after it's finished? What does this say about you?

Do you find that you are genuinely excited by the success of your mate, or is there a hint of jealousy? What does this say about your own feelings about yourself?

Do you resent the fact that your Adam or Eve never looks presentable enough in public? What does this say about your sense of shame or need for social acceptance?

Do you find your mate's hobbies silly? What does this say about what you consider important and meaningful? What does it say about your personality or your hidden feelings?

The mirror of your mate reflects you. If something your mate does makes you furious, you often have that trait inside you: you are really furious at yourself and are projecting that onto your mate. If something your mate does makes you joyful, you are seeing in your mate a trait in yourself that makes you joyful: you are projecting your own self-love onto your mate.

Sometimes your mate may do something that just ticks you off because it is like something your father or mother would do. If you respond by venting your annoyance, you will have missed a golden opportunity. Your mate is actually giving you the chance to let go of what's bothering you about your father or mother and free yourself from the past. Besides, you may actually notice that the way you behave toward your mate is just like your father or mother would behave. Reflecting upon the mirror of your mate can help you see yourself as you really are and not who you think you are or refuse to believe you might be. Reflecting upon the mirror of your mate is one of the most powerful ways to

help you de-program the automatic behaviors you learned
as a child, behaviors that may be preventing you from
expanding your freedom in God's Garden.

A true shared-soul marriage is a challenge. Each of the
partners holds up a reflection of God's own truth to the
other person. This is why marriage is often so difficult and
so contentious. It is impossible to escape the other person
because it is really impossible to escape yourself. You must
constantly look at yourself, question yourself, challenge
yourself. You must either choose to ignore what you see
(which, unfortunately, is the route a lot of fallen marriages
take) or you must choose to face what you see, reflect on
yourself, and make a conscious decision to grow and change.

In a shared-soul relationship, your partner is the single
most important teacher in your life next to God. It is
through your partner that God's most important lessons are
delivered right to your doorstep.

Now, when you think about it, this carries with it an
enormous responsibility. Unfortunately, many of today's
Adams and Eves do not take this kind of responsibility seriously, which is a major cause of our epidemic divorce rate.
It's also not always the kind of responsibility that is part of
more casual relationships, where people may just be living
together or sleeping together.

In a true spiritual marriage, God has actually designed
you to be the mirror for the other's own self-honesty. As a
shared soul, it's your job to correctly, objectively, and lovingly reflect the true heart and mind of your mate in order
to provide help and guidance. When he is lost, it's your job

to help him find himself. When she is confused, it's your job to help her find clarity. You are your mate's other half. You are the side, the rib of the shared soul that your mate cannot see. It's as if you are his other eyes, her other ears; you are the voice of the conscience he won't hear, of the conscience she's perhaps even forgotten she has.

As a shared soul, you have a responsibility to help your mate connect to God when he's lost his way— even if he is absolutely insistent that he knows what he's doing.

As a shared soul, you have a responsibility to lovingly remind your mate "how much better" she could be, "if only she would..."

As a shared soul, you are divinely appointed to assist your mate in exploring the full depth of your emotional, physical, and spiritual lives.

Needless to say, such an awesome task requires great skill. You are touching your shared soul on a level that only God touches. The tact, the kindness, the sincerity, the altruism you bring to the task must be impeccable—or as close to impeccable as possible, although none of us is perfect.

This is not always easy. When one mate is going through a problem, it can often threaten the other. It might rock the boat, forcing one mate to make changes that the other sees no need or perhaps has no desire to make. So, sometimes, the advice rendered back by a shared soul may be tinged with fear or self-interest: "Don't do that, because you'll do this to me." "You're making a serious mistake; it will damage our relationship."

As a shared soul, you must put such fearful self-interest aside. When you react with fear for self-preservation, what happens is that you actually get hooked into your mate's problem. You add your own problems on top of her (or his) problems and make it impossible for her to hear her own voice, which leaves you even more vulnerable than before. As a shared soul you are so close that you can actually smother your mate with just a sigh of criticism.

Your goal as a shared soul must always be to help the other see the light of God within her (or him) by being the purest possible reflection of that light to her. Helping your mate uncover her true feelings and re-establish her connection to God is the best possible way to assure that your interests and your fears will be considered. After all, you will be helping her align to God's order, which means she will also be aligned to you—since God's order includes you. Your interest is automatically taken care of when you take care of your mate because you are a shared soul. That's how the law of the Garden works.

In fact, if you pay very close attention to what happens in your shared-soul marriage, you will notice something magnificent. The events that occur between any Adam and Eve are exquisitely ordered and designed for the perfection of their individual souls through the perfection of their shared soul. Ninety-nine percent of the time (not a finely honed statistic), a change that one mate goes through actually forces the other person to make a corresponding change, and that change turns out to be exactly what the other person needed but, until that moment, wasn't aware of. The awareness often comes when long-married Adams or Eves look back with with 20/20 hindsight over turbulent events. Everything sort of falls into a pattern of understanding, and they can see God's hand in all the events in their shared life, no matter how challenging.

However, the purpose of adopting a shared-soul perspective is not to look backwards with understanding, but to actually be able to look forward with understanding. With a shared-soul perspective, you learn to approach any event that happens to you with an eye for how it can make both halves of the shared soul more aligned to God's order. You always try to see God's lesson in everything that is taking place for both of you while it is happening. This way, you are constantly approaching any challenge as a spiritual opportunity to grow closer to God and creation, and closer to each other as a single shared soul.

There is, however, one very, very dangerous pitfall in a shared-soul marriage. Indeed, it's the pitfall into which the poor, unsuspecting biblical couple fell under the subtle coercion of the serpent. It's also the same pitfall that created abusive marriages of the past, the types of marriages against which today's Adams and Eves rebelled. Although in a true spiritual marriage you are a shared soul, this does not mean that each of you is ever less of a soul. Although each of you helps complete the other, this does not mean that each of you is less complete. Although each of you contains each other's missing part, this does not mean that in either of you something is missing. What is missing is not a defect within you; it is simply a part of you remaining to be discovered. The purpose of a shared-soul marriage is to uncover that part within yourself by experiencing that part in the other. You should never degrade yourself for not already possessing it or envy your mate for having something you don't.

Moreover, being a shared soul should never become a crutch that enfeebles or infantilizes each other so that you cannot stand on your own two feet, unable to make a decision without relying on, clinging to, or even slobbering over your "better half." This is what will turn a joyful, totally dependent marriage into a dangerous co-dependent marriage, as contemporary psychologists call it. Nothing weakens a shared soul more than two partners who are not equally strong.

Before the rib was removed from the original Adam, God caused a deep, deep slumber to fall upon "him." In a way, we are all still asleep. We are not fully aware that somewhere in the Garden of God's consciousness is a shared soul from which every Adam and Eve was derived and recombined through marriage. So, the job of every married couple is simple: Wake up! Wake up to the shared soul you are. Wake up to the awareness that between you, and beyond you, is a greater soul, God's original handiwork, that defines the true purpose of your marriage and your individual lives.

Wake up to the fact that the person with whom you have chosen to share a life is actually yourself—in disguise.

MARRIAGE SECRET #8

Enjoy not being alone

Then the LORD God said,
"It is not good that the man should be alone."
(Genesis 2:18)

Why bother being married? Is it worth all the headaches, all the compromises, all the sacrifices? Do you really want to justify yourself to another person? Do you really want to be challenged by a mate?

These questions are so important that in the story of Adam and Eve it's actually God who supplies the answer to all of them. After observing Adam naming all the animals, but not finding a single one that was "his type," God, with great compassion, declares: "It is not good that the man should be alone."

This is not an idle comment, especially when you realize that the entire order of creation was designed to be good.

For God to declare Adam's solitary existence to be "not good" is like saying: "This is completely contrary to my intention for all of existence."

Why is it "not good" to be alone? Because there is nothing in creation that *is* alone. Creation and aloneness are diametrically opposed. Creation is teeming with "company." When you think about it, aloneness is the very undoing of the universe. Aloneness is the return of everything to nothing, the reversal of God's handiwork. To be alone is to essentially be non-existent, which is exactly how so many Adams and Eves feel when they can't find "the right person."

> It's not good to be alone because we are human beings designed with the capacity to love, share, and create—God's very own attributes. It's impossible to express God fully if we're alone.

> It's good to not be alone because with a true spiritual mate you are constantly urged, constantly challenged to express the image and likeness in which you're made. Your marriage helps you fulfill the very nature, purpose, and destiny of your soul.

It's also good to not be alone for less cosmic, and no less important, human reasons. When you're not alone . . .

You can talk into the wee hours.

You can hold hands.

You can nuzzle close to keep your nose warm in winter.

You can pass the fork and try what the other person ordered.

You can do something absolutely idiotic, and you'll have someone to laugh *with* you.

You can cry and have someone hold you.

You can go to the beach to just relax, not "pick up" people.

You can eat popcorn, and with a VCR, it's heaven at home.

You can enjoy that new-car smell together.

You can gain fifteen pounds and still feel adored.

Here's the most wonderful thing about a good marriage: not only is it a marvelous spiritual journey, which helps both of you come closer to God, but it's also a delight. Not only do you teach each other, but you can learn from each other while you're enjoying each other's presence. Indeed, heaven and earth come together in marriage: God's purpose and your pleasure.

Sadly, even after a few short years of being married, so many of today's Adams and Eves forget how good it is to not be alone. They become dulled by routine. They start seeing the other as fitting in to a lifestyle—like a cog in a machine. They lose the romance. They actually start living like single individuals in each other's presence, more like roommates than mates. Unfortunately, they quickly forget how to enjoy the presence of the other person.

When your enjoyment of each other begins to ebb, even if everything in your marriage looks perfect—your home, your careers, your perfectly balanced finances—an emotional hole is created. Over time, this hole can seriously undermine the foundation of your marriage and the love that brought you together. So it's absolutely critical: you must *never, ever* forget how to enjoy the presence of your mate. You must always be able to stop what you're doing, look lovingly into the other's eyes, and sigh, "Oh—it is so good, so very good, to not be alone, especially with you."

Here are five simple ways (there are many others) to not only enjoy the presence of your mate, but actually intensify it, so that you enjoy each other more and more with every year that passes.

Always remember to play.

God placed you both in the Garden to delight in its delights. In fact, the Hebrew root for the word "Eden" means "pleasure" or "delight." The Garden is there for your shared joy, your shared enthusiasm, and your shared bliss.

Sometimes adult responsibilities, especially the garnering and spending of money, seem to take over our lives. Work is frequently given priority over play and, without realizing it, Adam and Eve fall right into God's "punishment."

To enhance your enjoyment of each other, always remember to schedule in time for play. Do silly things together. Take off your shoes and run barefoot. Have a pillow fight. It doesn't matter how you play, as long as you play.

Play refreshes you. Play helps dissolve away cares and worries. Play helps you both connect to your spirits, and therefore automatically aligns you to God's order.

Encourage each other's innocence.

Apart from the relationship of mother and child, no other relationship is closer or more intimate than a marriage. Your mate is, or should be, the person who knows you best of all, the person with whom you should feel most natural, most yourself. Other relationships, those with relatives, bosses, children, and neighbors, require a certain formality: you always seem to have to wear some kind of mask.

But a really good marriage permits you to strip away the mask and be innocent. You can show each other the side of yourself that the world, with all its demands, doesn't get a chance to see. You can permit each other to be children in God's Garden and enjoy the innocent expression of each other's souls together. This is a special kind of enjoyment that you can experience only with your mate; it keeps your relationship special, set apart from others.

Allowing yourselves to feel like innocent children together is the easiest and most natural way to relate as children of God.

Give without keeping track.

Many couples in this "me-generation" are more concerned with what they are getting in a marriage than with what they are giving. They seem to have a set of unwritten demands for each other, demands that the other, like a trained poodle, is supposed to meet. This is one of the quickest ways to lose a sense of enjoyment in the other person, to turn the other's very presence into a curse.

But when you delight in giving and when you continue giving without keeping a mental accountant's ledger for tallying up who did what for whom, the selfishness of today's generation can dissolve away. Both of you become fountains of giving for each other. Both of you receive without ever having to ask. Your needs are so satisfied by the other that you naturally give your mate your full attention.

Adopt an attitude and practice of innocent giving, and the pleasures of the Garden will open to you without any labor or pain. The curse is reversed.

Look your mate in the eye.

When you speak to your Adam or Eve while you are alone together, or at a restaurant, or even in the presence of others, always try to make eye contact.

There is a special light—the soul's light—that comes from the eyes. Allowing yourself to bathe in it forges a deep spiritual connection between the two of you.

At first, it might feel uncomfortable to look your partner in the eye. There is an enormous intensity and naked vulnerability that is projected through the eyes. Direct eye contact can strip away all your defenses and pierce your heart. However, it is well worth practicing, and continuing to practice, until it feels comfortable. Nothing makes you more aware of the presence of your mate than looking at each other directly in the eye.

Change your routine—and keep changing it.

Routine can dull your feeling of enjoyment for each other. On the other hand, when you change the routine, you open up your marriage to excitement, newness, and a fresh experience as innocent children in the Garden.

So, always try to make sure there is a constant stream of surprises flowing between you. Pepper your day-to-day life with the unexpected. This will help keep you from taking each other for granted, from allowing marital doldrums to overtake you.

Tonight, when you're in bed, when the room is quiet and the cares of the world are drifting away, take a moment to listen to the sound of your spouse breathing. Listen to the sound of your partner's spirit exhaling . . . and inhaling.

When you feel your heart filling with love, just pause and send a small prayer to God: "Thank you for not making me alone."

For a happy marriage, repeat the prayer nightly, until death do you part.

MARRIAGE SECRET #9

Always know where you are

*But the L*ORD *God called to the man, and said to him,*
"Where are you?"
(Genesis 3:9)

After the eyes of Adam and Eve were opened, they quickly hid themselves from God out of fear. Then God called out: "Where are you?"

What a strange thing for God to ask. The answer would seem perfectly obvious: Adam and Eve were there in the Garden, the very Garden that God had furnished for them. So, why should God ask a pointless question like that? Perhaps it's not so pointless.

Think of the Garden of Eden, for a moment, not as an actual nature-garden, but as the mind of God, an environment of goodness beyond any conceivable mortal idea of goodness. Now, think of Adam and Eve as souls, little thoughts in the mind of God. When Adam and Eve were tempted by the serpent, obeying their own desires without considering their place in God's mind, they started hiding from God. They were no longer good, so God could not find them. They were no longer part of God's goodness, so God couldn't see them. "Where are you?" God called out. But Adam and Eve had fallen from grace. Grace, God's own awareness of them, could not find them, because Adam and Eve could not find themselves. They had lost their connection to their own souls, the part of God within them, and, therefore, they became lost to God.

Knowing where you are—where you stand in relationship to God—is a fundamental and critical spiritual principle for a happy married life.

*Knowing where you ar*e means constantly evaluating your own spiritual growth, staying aware of your shortcomings, so you can correct them.

Knowing where you are means staying alert to the direction in which you need to go in order to improve and grow closer to God.

Knowing where you are requires you to always seek to understand the meaning of the life lessons that God is presenting you with, to understand what God is saying to you through the events in your life.

Knowing where you are means always heeding your conscience, the voice of God within you. It is your conscience that connects your mind to God's mind. Your conscience is your guide. Continuously asking yourself the question, "Where am I?" is like using a little compass that keeps you pointed in the direction of spiritual north, or God.

However, because you are a shared soul, knowing where you are individually in relationship to God is not enough. Your relationship to God can never be separated from your relationship to your mate. You must always know the answer to the question "Where are you?" in relationship to your mate, because, as mirrors of each other's souls, that will also answer the question "Where are you?" in relationship to yourself. Indeed, it will prevent you from hiding from yourself, the first step to hiding from your mate or God.

Knowing where you are in relationship to your mate is not always easy. As we saw in the biblical story, after Eve was created, Adam and Eve developed a certain blind spot when it came to knowing each other. This was understandable, because after their shared soul was split, each developed a private world that the other was not able to penetrate. That's how Eve was able to do what she did without Adam knowing.

Today's Adams and Eves also have such a private world, and in today's marriages, where spouses are often considered individuals first and couples barely second, individual privacy is intensified. Certainly, there is a private world within each of us, a world that our spouse must respect, a special place in conscience for ourselves and God alone. However, when the need for privacy excludes a spouse, or becomes excessive, it can cause problems. This is especially common in couples who have had extensive single lives before getting married and are very set in their ways or used to their own space. Spouses may unintentionally withdraw from each other and lose track of each other, simply falling back into an old pre-marital habit as perfectly normal behavior.

Many an Eve of today often complains that Adam gets so shut up in his little world and is so unaware of what she needs that she "might as well live alone." Often, she just tolerates the situation, instead of confronting it and asking, "Adam, where are you?" Adam too can feel that Eve is so busy in her own little world that his desires are not being met. This is especially true now that Eve has joined the workforce and is often torn—or even shredded—between home and office. Adam might hold back his feelings in an effort to be extra nice and not tax Eve even more. However, what he should do is say, "Eve, where are you?" "Do you know where I am?"

Disconnections of this sort can occur between couples all the time. Sometimes it is just a momentary need for space on the part of one of the spouses. However, if it becomes chronic, and the two souls feel like they are going in completely opposite directions, this can precipitate a real crisis in the marriage. Remember, separation and divorce first happen emotionally; breaking up is usually the final stage in a process, the result of each of the partners having failed to assess where they were before there was a problem.

This little imaginary exercise can help you evaluate the state of your marriage by determining where you are so that you never end up hiding from each other:

> Picture the two of you as two ladders that are side by side, with the feet of the ladders resting on earth and the arms and rungs of the ladders going up toward heaven. These are your souls. The job of your souls, and of your shared soul, is for the rungs to move upward together.

> In your mind, try to imagine the positions of your ladders. Are the rungs matched up, so there can be movement between you and your mate? Can you step across from one ladder to the other, so there's easy communication and sharing?

> Or, in your mind, are the ladder rungs unmatched? Is it perhaps because one spouse has failed to live up to her spiritual potential and fallen behind the other? Is it because one spouse made a positive change in his life and left the other one, relatively speaking, behind? The real reason only you can know.

If, at any time, while checking in on the spiritual state of your marriage you notice your rungs becoming unmatched in your mind, it generally signals a problem. Then, you must stop and ask yourself:

Where are you?

What do we need to do to make our rungs match?

What do I personally need to do to make my rungs match yours?

What do I need to do to help you make your rungs match mine?

Using this ladder exercise, it's much easier to stay conscious of where you are as an individual and where you are as a shared soul. When your rungs are matched, and you are experiencing a shared increase in freedom, oneness, and goodness, you can be pretty certain that where you are is in good standing with God and each other.

If you don't keep the rungs of your ladders matched and don't readjust the rungs when they become unmatched, generally what happens is that some kind of "exile" will take place in your marriage; you will experience some "punishment"—perhaps a fight between you—some loss of freedom, oneness, and goodness. As in the biblical story, this punishment should be viewed as a lesson whose purpose is to get you to stop and question "Where are you?" Remember, in the Garden, you sow what you reap. When a problem occurs, you should always reflect on how you may have caused it through the misguided use of your divine creativity.

If you continue to work at knowing where you stand in relationship to God and where you stand in relationship to your mate, you will never have to hide from each other, let alone God. Your mind, your mate's mind, and God's mind will be cooperating together as co-creators. God's thoughts, and God's thoughts *as you*, will work together rather than against each other; your marriage will experience grace.

Then, on those few occasions when you do slip and lose your way and someone calls out "Where are you?" you will quickly recover your presence of self and respond: "I'm right here, honey, where I belong. And I'm glad that God, and you, were there to remind me."

MARRIAGE SECRET #10

Learn to be helpmates

I will make him a helper as his partner.
(Genesis 2:18)

When God paraded all the animals in the Garden in front of Adam, but Adam could not find one that was his own kind, God decided to make a partner that was fit for him, a "helper," or "helpmate," as it is sometimes translated.

However, the original Hebrew for this phrase is very curious: The phrase *ezer kenegdo*, (pronounced eh-tzair ken-egg-doe) literally means "his match"—the right fit of complementary talents and abilities, as any shared soul would have to be. But, just as with the English word "match," *ezer kenegdo* also has a sense of being an engagement of equals as in a boxing match: two equally matched wills, two equally powerful souls—competitors, with a strong potential for conflict.

To be each other's helpmates, to be fit for each other in the sense of *ezer kenegdo*, means that your relationship must embody two seemingly opposing qualities: You must be compatible, but you must also be contrary.

Ask your average marital experts what they think is the most important thing in a marriage, and oftentimes they will glibly say "compatibility." It is commonly thought that a compatible couple should be opposites; as the expression goes, "opposites attract." However, the attraction in a long-term marriage is not the same kind of attraction as that between the north and south poles of a magnet. Opposites tend to attract in fiercely magnetic relationships, such as wild love affairs, "flings," or the sexual-attraction stage of a relationship, when appearances pull you uncontrollably toward each other. But the bonds of a strong spiritual marriage are forged when similarities attract—a relationship "after their kinds," as Genesis expresses it repeatedly.

To be compatible means that you have a similar view of life, a similar lifestyle, similar needs and goals, perhaps even a similar family, religious, or socioeconomic background. Such similarity allows you to share a single home together with relatively little friction. After all, a bird could love a fish, but where would they live?

Put simply, compatibility means you get along with each other. There is room in your heart for the other person in your life. You're open to the other's personality, nature, even idiosyncrasies—and we all have an ample supply of those. You're compatible when you're amenable to listening and taking in what the other is saying, as well as fluid enough to adjust your life to any changes that may be required of you. You actually like each other, which, in a long-term commitment, can sometimes be even more important than loving each other, because romantic love can fade, whereas romantic "like" stays.

However, mere compatibility alone can actually be lethal for a marriage. Mere compatibility can shift the balance of power between two spiritual equals. An excess of compatibility can turn spouses into "yes-mates," whose tactic for getting along is simple: just giving each other exactly what is wanted twenty-four hours a day. This is not getting along; this is losing yourself. Compatibility alone can hook the other into serious dependency problems. One spouse can, without realizing it, become a substitute parent and end up playing some kind of strange role in an early childhood drama that the other is acting out unconsciously. Or, one overly compatible spouse can actually be put on a pedestal, adored and worshiped. In the guise of being a helpmate, a spouse can actually become an "addiction"—a partner in co-dependency, as contemporary psychologists call it—which makes the other partner weaker and inhibits his spiritual growth. In many seemingly compatible marriages, one spouse may actually hide behind the other, adoringly, and never let the real self emerge. Often, however, the real self is busy manipulating, in a passive-aggressive fashion, behind the scenes, wheedling to get what it needs. In the name of "compatibility," a constant undercurrent of stress can be placed upon the union.

To be each other's helpmates in the sense of *ezer kenegdo*, you must always remember to balance compatibility with contrariness. You must take the bold, decisive step to balance your receptiveness and openness to your mate with strong, solid resilience and opposition.

To be each other's helpmates means that you are supposed to oppose each other. The very nature of being a helpmate includes opposition. You are not supposed to be just a "yes-spouse," giving your mate exactly what he wants. You are supposed to be a "match," an equally powerful partner, the unrelenting voice of the aspect of his shared soul to which he may be blind. So, when your mate is doing something that is wrong—for herself, for himself, or for God's order—opposition is not only a necessity, it is a spiritual duty.

Many so-called "spiritual" people think just the opposite about opposition. They have been schooled by family or religion to avoid opposition, under the traditional assumption that it can destroy a marriage. You may see many an Adam and Eve mincing their words, making all sorts of nervous pleasantries, guarding their tone of voice, repressing their anger—all in an effort to make it appear that they have a "nice marriage." However, what they are actually doing is undermining their marriage.

You cannot be a helpmate if you are not able to freely oppose your spouse and if your mate is not going to honor you for doing so. Opposing our mates for the genuine purpose of helping them is one of the greatest spiritual gifts we can give. Your Adam or Eve may not like it at first, because no one likes to be challenged; no one likes to be told what to do, or what not to do. However, by opposing your mate you're doing a spiritual service that will accelerate the growth of your partner's soul.

Genuine spiritual helpmates welcome opposition from their mate rather than cringing at it. The opposition is viewed as a challenge to grow and better align themselves with each other and God's order. Well-intentioned opposition from a mate who has your (and his or her own) best interest in mind is blessed opposition. This is the kind of opposition that the biblical Adam should have demonstrated, had he not been dozing unaware while Eve was off with the serpent.

The dynamic balance between compatibility and contrariness, openness and opposition, resilience and resistance can be achieved, however, only if you pay close attention to your tone and manner. True spiritual opposition need not develop into conflict. However, more often than not, it is tone of voice and hidden messages of disdain, frustration, worry, or anger that interfere with the good effect of spiritual opposition.

Here are a few basic hints to help you, while opposing each other, keep from accidentally pushing one another's buttons:

> Try setting aside a specific place in your home where you can oppose each other—maybe two favorite chairs or some pleasant location inside or outside your home. This way the other person can

"get in the mood" for being opposed. Start with an invitation: "Honey, let's sit here, and discuss this." Make it pleasant.

Before opposing your mate, use loving language, such as: "Honey, I don't mean to interfere, but..." "Adam, you always asked me to be perfectly blunt with you. Well, I..." This will help take the edge off, and prepare your mate's ego for a challenge.

Avoid pat sweeping generalizations or judgments (my wife always detested mine) like: "You're wrong." Certainly avoid comments like, "You're an idiot" or "What? Are you crazy?"

Having set the tone, you are now ready to apply your full spiritual power as a helper. Helping is an art, and it takes a considerable amount of practice. It often happens that what may appear to be a help is really a hindrance, and knowing the difference can make all the difference in the world. Here are four basic guidelines; you will discover many more on your own as you put the art of being a conscious helpmate into practice.

Help in a way that strengthens—not weakens—your mate.

Remember, your purpose as a helpmate is to promote the spiritual growth of your partner. Therefore, when you help him, don't just do things for him. Don't try to fix things and always make it easier for him. This kind of "parent-style" help can actually keep him from facing himself and maturing as a spiritual being. Instead, help him in ways that help him to help himself. Help him to find his own answer, for there is always an answer to any problem residing in his soul. Your job as a helpmate is to simply help him look within and discover it.

Help in a way that allows your mate to make mistakes.

It is through mistakes, and even "punishments," that the biblical couple learned. You do your mate no service by over-policing her so she doesn't make any mistakes. Such over-policing is often really your own fear of how her mistakes will affect you, a fear that is expressed in the form of control. There is a certain vulnerability that you must always face in a marriage. Yes, your spouse will make mistakes and, yes, you will be affected by them and the consequences may not always be pleasant. That's just part of marriage. Stop fighting your fears of vulnerability by controlling your mate in the guise of helping. Since you have a totally dependent relationship in God's Garden, you're actually hurting yourself.

Help your mate in the way that he needs to be helped, not in the way you think he needs to be helped.

Ask your mate, "How can I help you?" Ask not just in terms of "What can I do?" but "How is it that you would like me to help you, in a way that encourages your spiritual growth most and feels most right to you?" Many mistakes in marriage are made by one spouse simply deciding, unilaterally, what is the "right way" to help the other. "The road to hell is paved with good intentions." This was one of my fortes, before I learned better. Remember, although you are a shared soul and may know a side of your spouse that he cannot fully see, he must ultimately be the judge for himself. She must feel that your "right way" is right for her. Otherwise, even with the best intentions in mind, you will be violating his or her free will. That's against the entire order of creation, and that will lead you both into exile, fast.

Help in a way that allows your mate to help you in return.

In general, the best way to help your mate is in a way that allows your mate to help you at the same time. Help has a way of enfeebling others and making them feel less independent. However, a mutual exchange of help between two partners empowers both and intensifies the shared-soul relationship between them. Because you are a shared soul, any time your mate needs help, chances are that you need it too, but you don't realize it at that moment. Stay alert to the fact that your mate's needs are often your needs in disguise, and for any help you give, don't be afraid to ask for help in return.

Being each other's helpmates is one of the most rewarding aspects of a true spiritual marriage. Nothing builds a stronger, more long-lasting bond between spouses than a couple composed of two committed helpmates. It's worth all the time and effort you will put into perfecting the art of helping.

God is always there to help you, too. However, why not start by trying to trust the helpmate who was placed there for you. You may find that all the help you need is right there. After all, your mate is your soul, that piece of God, that was made *fitting*—just for you.

God helps you all the time through your helpmate, if you're willing to help yourself by listening.

III
Banishing the Serpent

MARRIAGE SECRET #11

Don't listen to the serpent

Now the serpent was more crafty than any other wild animal
that the Lord God had made. He said to the woman,
"Did God say, 'You shall not eat from any tree in the garden'?"
(Genesis 3:1)

Who is this serpent, this beguiling creature? To many he is the devil, the voice in the Garden opposed to God. He represents the insidious presence of Satan, whose desire is to topple God's kingdom, casting souls into hell or, as the story describes it, physical existence—a hell for the fallen couple.

To others of a more psychological bent, the serpent is a symbol. The serpent has been said to represent our unconscious, the dark, fearsome, terrifying unknown, including the powerful, primitive lusts and desires that we all have deep within our psyches. The serpent has been said to be a phallus symbol with which Eve cavorts illicitly in some kind of ancient penis envy.

The serpent has also been said to represent our false egos, the self-contained arrogant child within us who feels so free—too free—to rebel against parental authority, whether God or an earthly parent.

From a biological perspective, the serpent represents the primitive reptilian brain that's embedded deep within our cerebrum. Our serpent-mind, like a reptile's, just reacts without any conscious or higher intelligence. It corresponds physiologically to the limbic system of the brain, the seat of emotion. The reptilian brain pales in comparison to the mammalian brain, with its higher rational abilities, and even more so to the human brain, with its supernatural conceptual abilities, including the capacity for conscious moral decision or spirituality. Similarly, many cultures worshiped a reptilian-like "nature god" before the Hebrews became a people and began worshiping a God with a higher intelligence, the Creator.

In a way, all of these views of the serpent are the same. In all of them, the serpent represents some kind of limitation: the devil limits God; unconscious chaos limits God's order; desires that drive the reptilian brain limit our moral sense; false egos, which place our desires above God's, limit our alignment to God's order; physical bodies limit our awareness of our souls; physical reproduction limits our pleasure through pain; a nature god limits the knowledge of our Supernatural God. So, it's not surprising that when Adam and Eve rebel, place their egos above God, are uncontrollably attracted to the fruit and fall into the painful hell of dominant/submissive physical life, including death—all of these things are linked to one spiritual mistake: listening to the serpent, the personification of limitation and the denial of God's limitless nature. Certainly a devilish mistake.

To listen to the serpent means to limit God—emotionally, spiritually, materially, and physically. To listen to the serpent means to limit freedom, oneness, and goodness in your life. When you listen to the serpent, you take the infinite potential of God's goodness and put some kind of block on it. You obstruct God's light, creating a shadow, some problem, some "exile" or "banishment" from the good Garden in which God has placed us. Listening to the serpent means that you, like the biblical couple, listen to a voice other than the voice of God's goodness; you deny the God-knowledge within your own soul. Listening to the serpent means that you place some kind of mortal power— the power of your anger, your fears, the beliefs of others, society's rules and regulations, some believed religious "have-to"—over the power of God.

Listening to the serpent...you may live in fear of your boss firing you, and sit behind the same desk your entire life.

Listening to the serpent...you may believe that you can't have someone who loves you for who you

are, and you may there-
fore never find someone.

Listening to the serpent . . . you may believe that you
must be like other peo-
ple around you to be
accepted, and never dis-
cover your true self.

Listening to the serpent . . . you may trust the opinion of your spouse more
than your own, and lose
your own identity.

The Bible's view is that it is not God who is the cause
of our problems, though many people curse God when
something bad happens or immediately declare their athe-
ism; the cause of our problems is *us*. Often without knowing we are doing so, we fall under the influence of some
serpent. We listen to some limited idea, some limited
belief, some limiting prejudice, some "false god" or devil
that prevents God's goodness from being fully expressed in
our lives. We admit some kind of serpent-thinking into our
consciousness, permit ourselves to be programmed by the
ways of the world or by voices of limitation or evil. Then
we live according to this thinking, make decisions based on
it, and sow and reap our problems.

Even if you believe in an actual devil (and not everyone
does), the devil can have little effect upon you unless you

succumb to him and thereby sow and reap his will instead of God's. It is you who are the major collaborator.

As discussed in the chapter on Marriage Secret #5, the ability to sow and reap is part of our divine inheritance as creative beings. We all have the ability to sow and reap the products of our thoughts, words, and actions, because we are created in the image and likeness of the Creator. However, along with this prodigious creative power comes enormous responsibility. As creators, we can sow for good or we can sow for evil. As creators, we can listen to God's goodness or, listening to the serpent instead, we can limit or even destroy God's goodness. Indeed, the fate of this entire world rests in our hands through our creative power to sow and reap.

In God's Garden, your thoughts, your words, and your deeds are all desires which, like the biblical couple's desires, enter into God's mind, interact with the laws of God's order, and return to you the fruit of your actions, the reaping of what you have sown. When your thoughts, words, and deeds are aligned to the freedom, oneness, and goodness of the Garden, you receive back greater freedom, oneness, and goodness. God will add goodness to the goodness you sow, and you'll reap even more than you would have through your actions alone. However, when your thoughts, words, and deeds are not aligned to God's nature, when you are listening to the serpent, then, like the biblical couple, you'll receive back pain, punishment, exile, or banishment.

Although God has placed the entire goodness of the Garden here for us to enjoy, we are often not conscious of how we are using our creative abilities and what we are sowing and reaping in God's mind. So, we create all sorts of problems for ourselves and the world, problems that God never intended; this is traditionally called "sin."

If you are currently experiencing problems in your marriage, no matter how complex the problems may seem, they are usually the singular result of sowing and reaping against God's order:

> You are sowing and reaping things that you think you want, but don't really want or, in fact, things that make you miserable, but that you think you love.

> You are sowing and reaping what you believe will make you happy, but your belief is false and what you reap does not really make you happy.

> You are sowing and reaping a life according to false values, rather than God's good values, and creating a living hell, but you believe the false values are true, and so you sow them generously.

> You are listening to the serpent's voice over the voice of God, grabbing what you want, without any thought as to what God wants for you or what God's order requires of you; you are living but lost, thinking you're fully alive.

If you wish to have a marriage that's aligned to the goodness of God's Garden, you must learn to become very conscious about what you sow and reap, both as individuals and as a couple. One of the best ways of going about this is to do an honest appraisal in your life of what is good (aligned to God) and what is not good (un-aligned to God), and try to understand what you are doing to create or contribute to sowing these problems for yourself.

Are you experiencing debt? Ask yourselves if there are ways in which you have sown and reaped the debt that you are experiencing. In what way are you misusing money or not using your creative talents?

Are you experiencing unreasonable jealousy toward your mate? Ask yourself in what way have you behaved wrongly toward your mate, sowing and reaping your fear that your partner might seek someone else, and masking that fear as jealousy.

Are you experiencing problems in a job you hate? Ask yourself if you are sowing and reaping desperation because you don't believe God is freedom and that God's grace will support you in a career move.

Are you experiencing sexual dissatisfaction in your marriage? Ask yourself what you believe good sex is. Perhaps you are sowing and reaping an illusion

that can never be attained. Are you listening to too
many sex experts and not your own heart?

When you have a problem, if you go deep inside yourself and commune with God, you will discover something
absolutely astonishing. If you ask God, "What did I sow
and reap to create this?" the voice within your own conscience will provide an answer. The answer will bubble up
to the top of your head, sometimes faster, sometimes
slower. It may take a while, but it will eventually come to
you. Oftentimes, the answer will make you realize that
what appears to be just a problem "on the outside" is really
a problem "on the inside." Some psychological serpent is
luring you away from an experience of goodness. You have
been, without realizing it, sowing and reaping your own
inner problems, making them manifest in your experience
of life.

Many an Adam and Eve are tired and exhausted
from overworking. What they don't realize is that
they *have chosen* to overwork. They are sowing and
reaping the belief, "If I overwork, I will have more,"
only to find they have less.

Many couples don't spend enough time with their
children. They are sowing and reaping the belief
that "Money is more important than time with my
kids," or, "My career is more important than my
family." Do their children believe this too?

Many Adams demand sex from their Eves the
moment they feel the urge, and are rejected by
their mate. They are sowing and reaping the belief
that "My urge is more important than Eve." Or,
Eve is sowing and reaping the belief that "Adam is
not free to be free, because I don't want to feel un-
free, like an object."

You may not realize it, but virtually every moment of
the day you are sowing and reaping the experiences that you
are having in your marriage and your life. Your thoughts,
words, and actions, together with those of your mate, are
going out into God's mind, and God is fulfilling your
desires, weaving your thoughts, words, and actions together
to create the shared experiences of your marriage. Your
positive experiences, if you think deeply about them, will
prove to have begun with your positive sowing on the level
of thought or desire. Your negative experiences, if you
think deeply about them, will prove to have begun with
your negative sowing, also on the level of thought or desire.
Indeed, Adam and Eve might discover that they have been
sowing and reaping the same problem, separately, without
realizing it, and their desires have produced a "double-
whammy."

When Adams and Eves discover that they've created a
problem from serpentine sowing and reaping, many of
them often feel tremendous remorse, or even emotional
paralysis. They don't know what to do or how to get out of
the problem. Like the biblical couple, they feel ashamed,

cursed, or abandoned by God. However, this is not necessary in a universe founded on freedom and new beginnings.
When you have sown and reaped a problem, all you need
to do is to reverse the curse by sowing and reaping just the
opposite of the problem:

> If you have sowed and reaped a financial problem
> through overspending, start sowing and reaping
> good fortune instead.

> If you have been ignoring your mate because you
> are obsessed with problems at work, defiantly
> throw off the problems, solved or not, and start
> sowing and reaping more time with your mate.

> If you are getting passed by for promotions because
> you are not vocal enough or are afraid of con-
> fronting your boss, remind yourself that your boss
> is not God. Practice sowing and reaping confidence
> ("with faith," as the word "confidence" means in
> Latin) and you'll notice you're not passed by.

Changing the pattern of what you have been sowing
and reaping can sometimes feel uncomfortable. Whether
or not a pattern is good or bad, as human beings, we tend
to get locked into habits. Change itself is something against
which we seem to have a built-in resistance, something we
even fear. Sowing and reaping changes can seem easier said
than done, but in God's Garden, it's really just the opposite:

In God's Garden, it's always easier done than said.

It's always much easier to muster up your courage and dare to "just do it"—to defiantly and decisively sow and reap a new Garden for yourself—rather than to sit there accusing yourself of having sown and reaped your past mistakes. In God's Garden you are free, once you realize you've made a mistake, to undo the mistake and sow afresh. Traditional religious language calls this "repentance," and it is the most powerful of tools against the serpent's temptation.

God's Garden is designed to be an unlimited Garden of delight for every Adam and Eve. Its nature is to provide for the continuous expansion of happiness. It's a joyous place in which Adam and Eve can sow, reap, and create, aligned to divine grace, every conceivable joy in their lives.

But, in a Garden that is so fertile that it responds to every thought, word, and action, all Adams and Eves must take responsibility for the seeds they are planting. As creators, you can create trouble in your life as easily as you can create happiness, and God gives you the freedom to do both.

So, in God's Garden, the general rule is: "Be careful what you sow and reap. You may just get it."

MARRIAGE SECRET #12

Never, ever blame

The woman whom you gave to be with me,
she gave me fruit from the tree, and I ate.
(Genesis 3:12)

After Adam and Eve's fall, God turns to Adam, and asks: "Who told you that you were naked? Have you eaten from the tree of which I commanded you not to eat?" To which Adam, avoiding his conscience and therefore God, answers: "The woman whom you gave to be with me, she gave me the fruit from the tree, and I ate." Adam isn't to blame; it is "that woman" who is to blame. No—actually it is God who is to blame, since God gave him that woman in the first place.

Then, God turns to Eve and asks her what she did. Eve responds, "The serpent tricked me, and I ate." Eve isn't to blame. The serpent is to blame; she was powerless and contributed nothing to falling into his snare. Besides, this too is God's fault, since God created everything in the Garden, including the serpent.

God doesn't buy this "passing the buck." God knows it is not Eve alone, Adam alone, or the serpent alone who is to blame. All of them participated in this event. All of them contributed to it. And, as in a marriage, all must share, simultaneously, in the consequences of it.

Blame is one of the worst traps that a marriage can fall into. Something takes place in the marriage, and one mate or the other quickly, decisively, and with "black and white" certainty points a finger at the other and accuses: "You did this. You are to blame." Then the other partner, reacting with a flare of defensiveness and rage, retorts: "I did not. You're to blame." Before you know it, both Adam and Eve are squabbling like little children, locked in a battle for supremacy, each trying to be right, each condemning the other as wrong, and both destroying the peace of their household, the love between them, and their shared alignment to God's goodness in the Garden.

However, having learned about the marriage secret discussed in the previous chapter, you should already know something about imputing this kind of blame. After all, in a Garden where we reap the fruits of our thoughts, words, and actions, it is not so very easy to glibly assign blame:

When something goes wrong and you feel it is something your mate has done "to you," do you search

your conscience for what you also may have thought,
said, or done to contribute to it?

Do you ever stop to wonder if you may have sown
something that influenced your mate to respond to
you in this particular way?

Do you ever stop to consider that the problem may
have a long history, one that may even precede
your marriage, and you both have been fertilizing
and reaping the fruit of the problem for years?

Because you are a shared soul, it is highly unlikely—
except perhaps in the case of a premeditated, intentional
desire on the part of one spouse to actually hurt the
other—that anyone is completely to blame, or completely
blameless, in anything that occurs in your marriage. More
often than not, marriage partners are generally caught in
some kind of house of mirrors: both are sowing and reaping and contributing to a problem with no awareness of
their contribution. Both believe that the problem is the
other person's rather than their own. It is this kind of house
of mirrors that Adam and Eve and the serpent got lost in,
until the light of God shattered the house of mirrors and
made clear where the blame should rest: with them all.

In the same way, whenever there is confrontation in
your marriage, it is absolutely critical that neither of you
react by laying blame on the other without first taking a
long, deep, hard look at your own self. You should examine

yourself in the light of God as it is reflected in your good conscience rather than an angry house of mirrors. If each of you does this, more often than not you will find that it is not one spouse or the other who is to blame. Rather, the situation is usually the result of a dance, a comedy of errors, a combination of mutual falsities and confusions. You'll also discover that blame is a much more complex thing than simple-minded finger-pointing. It's not at all as "black and white" as most Adams and Eves believe.

In God's Garden it is very important to distinguish between three different concepts that are always getting tangled in our minds and marriages. The first concept is *blame*. Blame has to do with direct intention, and sometimes malice. Let's say someone deliberately decides to hurl a baseball through a window, just for fun or to enjoy the sound of a window breaking. The second concept is *responsibility*. Let's say someone has decided to play baseball by a window, and the ball accidentally goes through the window. The baseball player is really not to blame, because it was not an intentionally malicious thing, though the person might have been more cautious. However, the baseball player is certainly responsible; it's up to that person to be "response-able" and respond with appropriate recompense. The third concept is *innocence*. Let's say someone has never played with a baseball before, and didn't even know that a baseball was hard enough to go through a window, or that a window could actually break; that person is innocent.

In the Garden of Eden, the original couple was simultaneously innocent, responsible, and to blame. They really did not know what they were doing; having never experienced free will before, they were testing the limits of God's order. Yet, despite their innocence, God held them responsible for what they did. They were to blame because they had been forewarned about eating from the Tree of Knowledge—and they suffered the consequences for their action.

However, for today's Adams and Eves, innocence, responsibility, and blame don't always coincide so snugly. Unfortunately, we tend to lump them all together under one big umbrella of "blame" without looking more discerningly at what actually happened.

If you do look more discerningly, you'll sometimes find that your spouse can be blamed for something, but may have done it innocently, or sometimes your spouse can be totally responsible, but not at all to blame. Making yourself aware of these distinctions can help you from being so "black and white" and categorical in your finger-pointing.

Indeed, it is almost impossible for any human being with a finite mortal mind to perfectly determine who is to blame, who is responsible, and who is innocent. Even the wisest of judges in our judicial system can hardly claim perfect judgment of blame, responsibility, and innocence. Generally speaking, the most anyone can hope for is "the most wise" decision, a good relative judgment, not an absolutely good judgment.

The fact is that no human being can really know the complete depths of another person's soul. No partner in a marriage, no matter how close, no matter how much of a shared soul, is capable of fully knowing what motivates the other to do something. There is a certain inner privacy to your mate's soul that only God—and no one else—can penetrate completely. Besides, we are all a product of learning and conditioning. All of us have learned from generations past things that are wrong and, not knowing any better, we've innocently repeated the same mistakes.

Therefore, when you blame a partner without inquiring into whether he is really to blame, or just responsible, or merely innocent, you are essentially making yourself the judge of your spouse's soul. You are making yourself God—and that is one of the fastest ways to un-align yourself to God's order and be banished from Eden as a result. In fact, it is precisely this kind of self-righteous, god-like self-importance that is the major cause of an angry response on the part of your spouse to any accusation you make. It will often be the case that your mate is not reacting to the fact that you believe she did something wrong, which she may quickly admit to. More often, she is reacting to the fact that you are cruelly judging her without knowing all the circumstances, and that your tone of voice is categorical, judgmental, or even cruel.

You cannot judge your mate completely. You cannot judge any person completely. There is only one judge, only one standard by which behaviors can be correctly assessed as "good" or "evil": God. Indeed, that is the whole point of the story of Adam and Eve. They fall the moment they set themselves up as the standard of what they should do or not do. They fall the moment they cease to obey God's order by setting themselves up as judges of good and evil.

Since all spiritual couples are a shared soul and are totally dependent on God, creation, and each other, can we really ever separate ourselves blamelessly from what any one else does? Can we really assign blamelessness to ourselves and blame to our mates?

Lois complains that Max isn't paying attention to her. Does she ever notice that she is always shrill and irritating and constantly complaining?

Bernie blames Sharon for telling his parents to come over on Sunday, when he wanted to play football. Does he ever question why he has made Sharon the go-between with parents with whom he has had a strained relationship that hasn't been healed?

Toby thinks Becky is overspending, and Becky thinks Toby is just plain cheap. Do they ever stop to think about where each of them actually learned their attitudes toward money, rather than blame each other?

All too often, we blame the person. However, no person lives in a vacuum. We are all a bodily collection of beliefs, ideas, thoughts, programs, learned experiences, inherited personality traits, cultural and religious attitudes—all of which influence our behavior in any given situation. If you look past the surface of any action, you will often see that there is a huge, talking serpent in your spouse's mind or yours. There is some kind of very powerful, persuasive belief system that is really the culprit in any problem between you. One spouse or the other is so absolutely certain about the way things should be done—"That's how my mother did it"—or they are so absolutely unconscious about why they do what they do, that they are just acting without thinking. In either case, they are listening to the serpent, responding automatically and reactively and, therefore, like the biblical couple, exiling themselves from the presence of goodness.

When there is an argument between you, always try to look past the skin of your spouse. Under that skin is a human soul who has, whether he is aware of it or not, been strongly influenced by serpentine thinking that he has accepted as true and acted upon, thereby sowing and reaping his share of most every argument between you. He may have picked up the thinking from friends or relatives, society or church. Wherever it has come from, it is that thinking that is really to blame, not the person. It is that thinking that should be looked at, judged, examined, thought about, corrected, condemned, or improved on, so you will never again sow and reap the same problem for yourselves.

However, under no circumstances blame the person. If you have to blame, blame only the behavior. Don't blame your spouse's soul—her personhood. Remember that you are not the absolute judge of the human heart. You are well within your bounds to discriminate between a good action or a bad action of yours or your mate; in fact, you *should* do so, no less than the biblical couple should have. But any such discrimination is human discrimination. It is made with a finite mind, which is only a bite of God's knowledge, not the whole tree. You must never pretend to take on the kind of absolute knowing that must be reserved for God and God alone.

Freeing yourself from excessive judgments can transform your marriage from hostility to humility, from belligerence to beauty, because you will open yourselves up to one of the most powerful spiritual forces in creation, a force that can free you from the serpent's hypnosis and liberate you both from the house of mirrors called "blame." That power is forgiveness.

Forgiveness isn't just "making up." It's not just ceasing to blame someone after you have already blamed her. This is a twisted misunderstanding of a wonderful spiritual power—a power so strong that, according to the Bible, it's an actual attribute of God.

Forgiveness is really the releasing of any wrong that has been done—a letting go of the incident. Even if there is hurt involved, or suffering, true forgiveness, when it is granted, means that you both acknowledge that whatever happened between you was simply the result of being children of God on a difficult learning curve where mistakes, because we are human, are inevitable. Forgiveness is a mutual acknowledgement of your mutual place in creation, and is therefore a form of humility, a shared reminder that you are both dust.

Forgiveness is one immensely powerful giant step past blame, past responsibility, and past innocence. Forgiveness repairs all the mental confusion about who did what to whom. After all, the only mistake most of us ever make is simply not knowing enough to do better. Whom can we blame for that? God? Or ourselves, for not listening to God?

The road back to Eden is paved with forgiveness, so never, ever blame.

MARRIAGE SECRET #13

Think before you act

You may freely eat of every tree of the garden;
but the tree of the knowledge of good and evil you shall not eat.
(Genesis 2:16–17)

When Adam and Eve took a bite of the "apple," they received knowledge of good and evil. Why an apple? The Bible doesn't say what kind of fruit it was, but it just so happens that the word for "bad" in Latin, *malus*, is the same as the word for "apple," and after many centuries of interpretation that's how the story's been told.

God told Adam and Eve that once they ate such a "bad apple" they would die. The serpent, however, said that they would not die, but would become "like gods." In a way, they were both right; the serpent didn't lie, but simply manipulated God's truth: Adam and Eve became immortal, but their immortality was now achieved through birth and death, generation after generation, dying and being born. Their immortality was now a group immortality—not a personal immortality—for God withheld the Tree of Life from Adam and Eve presumably until they gained the knowledge to be worthy of it. Adam and Eve, two sides of the one soul of humanity, became two individual human beings, enfleshed in "animal skins," living and operating in the real, physical world of the Garden we live in today.

It is in such a real, physical Garden—not just the metaphysical Garden of souls-as-thoughts in God's mind—that earthly marriages take place. In this kind of world, the spiritual laws that God lays down before us are even more complex than the simple "don't touch" that the biblical couple failed to obey. Why? Because in a real, physical Garden, there is considerably more at stake if something goes wrong. In a real, physical Garden, bodies can undergo pain, suffering, and untimely death. In a real, physical Garden, emotional scarring can take place, scarring that can perpetuate cycles of marital abuse, generation after generation. In a real, physical Garden, sexuality can be cruel and can violate the physical integrity and conscience of another human being. In a real, physical Garden, God's creativity, as expressed through the organic human species, can be destroyed if human beings go astray.

This brings today's Adams and Eves back to a subject which they often balk at: morality. These days, there's a lot of talk about spirituality, but there is a general unwillingness to discuss morality. Even saying the word "morality" can make some young couples bristle. Part of the reason for this is that many misguided clergy in the past turned the matter of morality into a tool to make couples feel guilty and control them. Also, today, morality has often become a cruel, "finger-pointing" religious/political weapon that often seems to create more divisiveness than oneness, leaving a lot of intelligent people questioning if it is really from God. However, just because there are some who misrepresent morality, or represent it in morally questionably ways, does not mean that morality itself can ever be dispensed with. Next to God, morality is the cornerstone upon which a good, healthy marriage is built. And, because all human institutions are built on the foundation of marriage, morality is also the pillar that supports the structure of all human life and civilization.

The basic principle of morality, as Adam and Eve shamefully discovered in the Garden, is very simple: *Think before you act.* You are not alone. You are not the Creator of the universe. There is an order here. So, before you decide to just make up your own rules and act, consult your conscience, listen to God's voice—think before you act.

Such a simple principle is often forgotten in marriages. It often happens that couples are far more moral, far more polite, far more gracious to each other before getting married than afterwards. Before marriage, we are often on "good" behavior. Anxious to impress the other person, we often appear to be fine specimens of moral virtue, thinking carefully, measuring our words and actions before we speak or do something. However, after getting married, a certain flimsy familiarity sets in. We now live with the other person; we hear their toilets flush and their phlegm clear; we see them—horror of horrors—after waking up. The marital joy of finding someone we can totally relax with often degenerates into a situation in which we feel we can say or do anything we please, expecting the person who signed on the dotted line to tolerate it because they're "stuck with us." I need not go on about this. Everyone has seen long-term married couples who act so familiar with each other that they might as well be street acquaintances rather than shared souls born of God.

Marriage is a holy relationship, the union of two sparks of God's own light. Thinking before you act is not just a guideline for dating, but is a sacred principle that must be learned and acted on through every year you're together. This is not to diminish the joys of relaxing with each other, feeling free and familiar, but only to keep proper moral bounds of mutual respect that are an essential part of the spiritual relationship between spouses.

Thinking before you act requires you to do something that does not always feel natural. Indeed, it is not natural, it is super-natural, which is why for an innocent child, or for the newly created Adam and Eve, it is difficult to do. Thinking before you act requires you to separate your mind from your heart.

Your mind and your heart feel aligned when you desire something. Your mind says "yes" and your heart says "go for it" and the two work together to produce a single impulse that propels you toward satisfying that desire. But such a feeling of alignment doesn't necessarily mean that your mind and heart are naturally aligned to God's order. You can be aligned merely to your own desires, and not God's, which include yourself, your mate, all humanity, and all creation. For instance, you may desire to shove a piece of chocolate cake into your pre-diabetic body; that's destructive of God's creation, which *is* your body in physical form. You may desire to cruise bars and sleep around promiscuously; that can seem fun at first, but may end up depleting your spiritual/sexual energy, lowering your self-esteem, or exposing you to terrible diseases. Even if your desire is good, you can go about fulfilling that desire in a way that is not morally good. For instance, you might want to enhance the beauty of your home with a bouquet of flowers, so you just take them from someone else's garden without asking. You might want to be amorous with your spouse when he's not in the mood, and you force him against his will.

Morality means that you can't operate just on the innocent level of desire, touching and picking the fruit you want without thinking. Desires may feel free, but they are not necessarily spiritually free. As a spiritual adult, you have to separate your mind and your heart, and in the small space between them, your conscience, you must ask yourself some very important questions:

Does what I desire create the greatest freedom, oneness, and goodness for my mate, myself, and my world?

Does what I desire help me, but not my mate? My mate, but not my world? My world, but not us?

If what I desire does not create the maximum freedom, oneness, and goodness for all, how can I change my desires or the way I go about satisfying my desires so that I can act in the most moral way possible?

To think before you act means to just pause and give yourself a moment to reflect on God before you do something, to train yourself to make moral decisions that will benefit your spouse and all the different aspects of creation. To think before you act means incorporating consideration, if not caution, so that your action becomes a blessing, and never a curse.

However, this does not mean you must spend your life split between mind and heart, monitoring everything you do, worrying, fretting, and even panicking over whether you are doing right or doing wrong. This so-called religious behavior is not true morality. It has been contaminated with obsession/compulsion and it's the dark side of moral discretion. It happens when the mind not only separates from the heart for reflection, but dominates the heart totally, extinguishing it, so that every decision is weighed on a mental scale, without any respect for feeling. Such obsession/compulsion generally results when people have a notion of God that is so fear-ridden, so fire-and-brimstone, that they live in mortal fear of making the slightest mistake.

It is this kind of "morality" that so many of today's Adams and Eves have thrown off, because in the past it was cold, cruel, disrespectful of individual differences, and destructive of spontaneity and human joy. It was also especially male-dominated and controlling of women.

You do not have to go about feeling split in order to learn morality. Miraculously, God has designed the Garden to actually help instruct every Adam and Eve on the art of moral discretion. Indeed, that was purpose of the fall into flesh. Our physical world has been designed to teach us proper moral boundaries, automatically, as long as we don't fall asleep to its lessons.

The Garden is the best instructor of morality because every person in it and, in fact, every thing in it, on some level reflects yourself and provides you an opportunity to learn about yourself. The same house of mirrors into which the Garden degenerates when you've lost your connection to your soul can become a true mirror that reflects right action and correct moral behavior when you stay aware of your soul and the lessons God places in front of you:

> If you yell at your spouse, you can witness pain and anger. Now, seeing yourself in light of that pain and anger, what can you learn about correct morality? What should you have done? Was there another way besides yelling?

> You arrive home from work hungry, and you run into your kitchen, right to the refrigerator, and

ignore your spouse, who is hurt. Now, seeing yourself in light of that hurt, what can you learn about
correct morality? Should you have held back your
hunger instinct for a higher moral purpose?

To spiritual seekers who stay awake so they can see
events in their lives as reflections of themselves and are
willing to learn from those events, the Garden is a superb
teacher of morality. It is possible to learn not just personal
morality between you and your spouse, but also group
morality between you, your community, and the world:

If you litter on the street, you can see the filth on
the street. Now, seeing yourself in the reflection of
that filth, what can you learn about your community morality?

A business indiscriminately buys up the natural
resources of a poor country. Three years later, our
country must give that country financial aid. Now,
seeing ourselves reflected in the other country's
impoverishment, what can we learn about business
and government economic policy?

If you stay awake to how your actions affect other people and see yourself reflected in them, the real physical
Garden will automatically tutor you on correct differentia-
tion of right from wrong. In general, the moment you
overstep some intuitive moral guideline, you will notice

some unsightly reflection of yourself, you will experience some pang of conscience. When you do, that's the moment you need to stop and gently separate your mind from your heart, taking a moment to reflect on what you did to create or contribute to the problem. That's the moment you need to listen to the higher mind, God's voice in the Garden, realize your mistake, and then turn away from the serpent in the direction of good. In this manner, you become conscious of your mistake, so you can learn about moral boundaries and never make the same mistake again.

Morality learned in this kind of spiritual relationship with God and God's order is a living moral system that will not become old and brittle, that will never need to be dismantled and rebuilt. It is a breathing, spiritual way to learn about correct moral principles through the process of life. With every experience that you reflect upon and learn from, your moral sense will continue to grow, and grow stronger, strengthening your relationship with your spouse, with other people, and with all life in the Garden.

Over time, as you learn how to think before acting and remember to think *after* acting when the Garden reflects a mistake, these lessons will become part of you. They will enter into your very life as individuals and as a couple and become second-nature to you. They will imprint themselves upon your souls. These consciously learned lessons will become subconsciously accepted and eventually automatic behavior. You will no longer have to think as much before you act. The thinking before you act will be built in.

Then, something marvelous will happen. You will begin to notice that the knocks and pitfalls your marriage has gone through in the past begin to soften. As you sow and reap naturally, but with moral precision, in loving consonance with each other and all life, the consequences of everything you sow will return to you a harvest of blessing after blessing. Indeed, you will notice a generous, loving, moral spontaneity infusing itself into your marriage.

Now you have innocence restored, but with moral wisdom. Congratulations. You've achieved the spiritual purpose of Adam and Eve's "exile" into the flesh. The Garden has taught you well.

MARRIAGE SECRET #14

Don't judge by appearances

So when the woman saw that the tree was good for food,
and that it was a delight to the eyes ... she took of its fruit and ate;
and she also gave some to her husband, who was with her, and he ate.
(Genesis 3:6)

You would have thought that Eve could have resisted the apple. After all, she knew, presumably from Adam (though the Bible doesn't say he told her) that God didn't want her to touch it. But, alas, her will power was not strong enough. Seeing the fruit of the Tree of Knowledge, she was drawn to it, teased by it, and seduced by it. It was so beautiful to look at, so scrumptious in appearance, that she lunged for it and plucked the forbidden fruit.

What had appeared to be a delicacy, enticing to eat, turned out to be just an appearance—a superficial sham, the serpent's scam; now humanity would be bound to physicality. Drawn to the superficial appearance of the apple, Adam and Eve fell into the superficial appearance of physical bodies; their uncontrolled animal-lust at the sight of something delicious led to their fall into "animal skins."

The lesson is clear: uncontrolled desire, based just upon our attraction to superficial appearances, results in our fall into lower, less spiritual states—an enslavement to, rather than an enjoyment of, our physical natures and material life.

Judging by appearances is one of the most lethal mistakes in marriages. It's a mistake that begins from the moment you start dating:

Eve judges Adam's potential for income by the car he drives.

Adam judges Eve's sexual openness by the clothing she wears or doesn't wear.

Eve judges Adam by the decor of his bachelor apartment; she rates her success as a woman by whether he seems a "good catch."

Adam judges Eve by how other men's heads turn when he walks down the street with her; he wears Eve like an ego-trophy.

In today's Garden, judging by superficial appearances has actually become a cultural norm, though it is questionable whether it should ever be considered spiritually normal. Today's Adams and Eves are so media-intoxicated, so addicted to style and appearances, that they are literally infected by the power of their senses. Meaningless criteria for attraction to a mate are given cosmic importance; meaningful criteria, such as the following, are squelched:

Is this person genuinely kind?

Does this person have habits I am comfortable with?

Can this person help me grow spiritually?

Am I valuable to this person as more than a sex tool?

Do we have similar values?

Over the long term, is this person going to bore me?

What is my spiritual gift to this person?

Does God want me to be with this person?

Judging by appearances is certainly part of the natural attraction that's one of the delights of the Garden. However, when other more important judgments are dwarfed because they are overwhelmed by the luring appearance of the "apple," you can make some serious mistakes. Not a few people, having been attracted to the other based upon superficial allure, wake up one day only to realize that the person they thought they had married is not the person they actually married.

How does this happen? It's the serpent's hypnosis: you fall in love with the other person's superficial aspects that you consider symbolically important to you. You interpret the meaning of these superficial aspects according to your own value system—but not according to God's—and then plunge into the relationship. In essence, you fall in love with *your own idea* of a mate—a reflection of your own deluded mind or psychological problems. The outer appearances to which you are attracted are really symbolic of your inner needs, which you project upon the other person:

> You are attracted to a partner with money, but it is you who need money, because you may have grown up poor, or are addicted to money, or because you grew up rich.

> You are attracted to a partner who turns out alcoholic because you desperately need to find the missing love of some parent who was alcoholic.

> You are attracted to a partner who is strong and powerful because no one was there to guide you when you were growing up and you felt lonely or lost.

> You are attracted to a partner who is a "wet noodle," someone you can boss around, because you

always felt weak and controlled and this gives you
an opportunity to feel a powerful ego's confidence.

When you are married to the outer appearances of
someone because there is a hole inside you, you have set
yourself up for a real problem. The appearance of the person is like the apple; it lures you and addicts you. You seek
the completion of yourself by trying to "ingest" the other
person, rather than by looking deep inside you to fill your
spiritual hole. Trying to fill a hole by "eating" an aspect of
the another person is at best only a temporary solution; as
in all addictions, the craving returns, and returns stronger,
the more you feed it.

Judging by appearances can seriously undermine your
shared life together:

Make a career move based on the superficial appearance that you'll have more money or power, and you
can end up working twice as much, and having less
to show for it, alienating your mate at the same
time.

Instead, ask yourself: Do I enjoy this kind of
work? Do I like the feeling in the office, and
the people I will be with? Are their values God-
based? Can I grow spiritually from this work?

Buy a house based upon superficial appearances so
you can impress your relatives or neighbors, and
you could end up exhausting yourself to pay the

mortgage, dumping all the pressure on your mate and never being able to enjoy your home.

Instead, ask yourself: Can I relax in this house? Will this house help increase my energy, so that I can accomplish important things like expressing my creativity or enhancing my spiritual growth? Is there a spiritual reason to buy this house?

Judging by appearances can wreck the communication in your marriage. When you judge by appearances, you'll leap to conclusions about your mate's behavior, conclusions based on superficial understanding and your own personal anxieties or phobias. Thus, you'll often misinterpret your mate. Instead of seeing the true motivations for your mate's behavior, you'll react blindly in response to the "buttons" your mate pushes in you.

Bettina noticed that Rick had gotten very sullen lately. He was spending a lot of time alone and ignoring her. She believed it was due to the fact that she had gained twenty-five pounds and was no longer as attractive as she had been. Actually, it was because at his office there had been changes that were threatening his job. He hadn't told her about the changes because he didn't want her to worry.

Max got very angry at Roberta when he found out that she had purchased $300.00 of what he considered "frivolities." He didn't say anything to her about it, but he assumed that she had simply decided to ignore their household budget. His greatest fear had always been that he would marry a woman who would end up being extravagant like his mother. Actually, Roberta had received a gift from her parents, and was simply enjoying a "perk." She hadn't mentioned the gift to Max because she knew that he would have wanted to use it for "house things," like new tools and paint for the garage, rather than "fun things," like decorating.

These are the kinds of communication knots that are created when you judge by appearances. The solution to judging by superficial appearances is to simply look below the surface. For instance, in the first example, ask your mate directly, face-to-face: "Do you feel I am ugly now that I've gained twenty-five pounds? Is that why you are ignoring me?" This gives your mate a chance to answer: "No, honey. I'm worried about the office. Now that you're twenty-five pounds heavier, I just have more to love." See how quickly the paranoia that results from judging by appearances disappears if you're brave enough to confront your superficial judgments head-on?

This is a win-win technique, because even if the answer were to be "Yes, honey, with those twenty-five extra pounds I'm not as turned on by you," at least you'd know the truth. Then you could maturely decide what to do about it: either lose weight or seriously confront your helpmate for judging you too much by appearances.

If you are in a situation that makes you feel very uncomfortable and you cannot, for whatever reason, directly confront your spouse about superficial judgments, then it's best to take a moment to connect with God and seek some counsel from deep within yourself. If you are open to a voice of higher knowledge, and you don't allow the serpent's voice to drown it out, you will find that a clear, lucid "knowingness" begins to pool up within you that will wash away many of your misconceptions. The emotional or psychological issues that may be causing you to use superficial appearances to misread your spouse will become clearer. You'll have an opportunity to look more deeply into your soul and clear out the garbage—your fears, angers, early childhood programming, etc.—contaminating your perception of your spouse. This will help you to see your mate more clearly, not as your projection, but as who that human being really is.

In this way, over time, you and your spouse can actually begin to develop spiritual senses. You will begin to see, hear, touch, and smell differently. You will judge not just with your superficial senses, but with the higher mind behind your senses. Instead of relying on the primitive part of your brain that judges reactively by superficial appearances, you'll begin to gain use of your spiritual mind, which is more aligned to God. Your spiritual intelligence will amplify your senses and allow them to penetrate more deeply into the heart of things. Indeed, slowly, with practice, you will begin to acquire a genuine sixth sense for discerning the truth in any situation. You'll realize the powers of your intuition, a very special spiritual faculty. Then you will no longer be lured by superficial appearances or by the serpent's coercion. You will have a true, authentic God-sense of what is right or wrong or true about your mate.

Creation begins with the Invisible God, not with visible forms. Spiritual substance comes before superficial appearance. Judging by superficial appearances leads to a fall because it reverses the order of creation. When you judge by superficial appearances, you put the result before the cause, the consequence before the intention, the created before the Creator, the reaping before the sowing, the fruit before the tree, the serpent before God. You actually turn back God's handiwork, reversing the entire flow of the universe through your superficial judgment, setting up a "wake" that will rock your marital boat.

So, even if you see the most perfectly bred apple shimmering in front of your eyes, even if the most transparent, crystalline dew-drops are glistening on its voluptuously shiny red skin, even if your throat begins to contract and your saliva begins to flow with unremitting desire at the sight of it:

Don't bite! Appearances are deceiving.

MARRIAGE SECRET #15

Don't let doubts creep in

I will put enmity between you and the woman
and between your offspring and hers;
he will strike your head, and you will strike his heel.
(Genesis 3:15)

Having tempted Eve to disobey God's order, the serpent was due for a punishment. God acted swiftly and decisively: the talking serpent, this powerful god of nature who had beguiled Adam and Eve into disobeying their supernatural conscience, was reduced to a groveling snake, dragging his belly across the dust forever. The serpent was returned to the very dust from which Adam had been formed, the humblest material in creation. Now he was lower than Adam, for the dust-born Adam had personally received God's breath of life.

God put the serpent in his place. The haughty, hypnotic serpent became a mere "garden snake." No longer as powerful, he would just "strike [Adam and Eve's] heel," while humanity would "strike his head." Human beings, now fleshly beings in the Garden, would have to begin their climb back to paradise consciously learning, through fleshly experience, what they had failed to learn as mere souls.

However, now that they were no longer souls in God's mind but physical beings, they would not have the same idyllic peace of mind as before. They would be vulnerable to a well-known viper: doubt.

The story of Adam and Eve tells us that, in some fashion, all our doubts are just by-products of the fact that we are created beings. Our doubts are little reminders of the limitations, the finiteness, and the constraints of humans. Life in the body constantly tempts us to forget that we are God's own children, that we are super-natural beings created in the image and likeness of God, souls as thoughts in God's mind. Our doubts constantly make us think that we are merely "ascended apes," doomed to experience the pain, suffering, and dominance/submission of animals, rather than the heavenly bliss of the "descended angels" whom we more accurately resemble.

Doubt cripples our spiritual natures. It is also snake venom in a spiritual marriage.

Doubt is insidious. Like a snake, it creeps up on you when you are unaware. Everything can be going right, you can be feeling good, and then all of a sudden the fanged betrayer of your spiritual confidence nips at your conscience:

"Adam's mind is always on his work. Maybe I'm not attractive anymore."

"Eve seems to be so busy with the children. She has no love left for me."

"Wow, I saw this incredibly sexy man today. Why did I look? This couldn't happen if we were *really* happy."

"Now that Eve has every material thing she ever wanted, she is no longer as affectionate with me. Maybe I'm not as good a lover as her first husband after all."

The list goes on and on. But notice the strange little structure to doubts: you observe something, such as "Adam's working hard," and then link it to another thing, such as "my attractiveness." The sight of a sexy man is linked to a preconceived idea of what a happy marriage is. All doubts have this kind of construction to them, and it is important to become aware of it.

Doubts are little conclusions that your mortal, apple-bite-educated mind creates. They are tiny little whispers, bugs in your ear. They always consist of some kind of judgment as to cause and effect. Using very scanty information you come to a conclusion that links two separate things. Adam's behavior is due to you, not him; it's something you did wrong.

However, underneath a judgment based on such scanty information is usually a tremendous amount of emotion. Eve may be angry about Adam working so hard and taking time away from her. Eve may also be depressed lately about growing older and not feeling very pretty. This may have nothing at all to do with Adam's work or how he feels. In the vast majority of cases, doubts are not due to the relationship itself. They are due to feelings within one or the other of you that color the events you experience and cause you to interpret those events in a way that undermines you, your spouse, or both of you.

When this takes place, the situation, now colored by doubt, will usually grow in force. The little garden snake will strike at your heel and the venom will spread to your mind. For a while, the problem may seethe quietly. Then it may eventually erupt into a full-fledged argument. This is a blessing in disguise, for such an eruption often provides a badly needed opportunity to clear the venom from your system.

The little conclusions created by your doubting might have some basis in reality or they might not. Doubts may point to real or imagined problems, but either way it's irrelevant. All doubts, to some extent, indicate some kind of wound to your spiritual nature, perhaps a deep wound from childhood, a wound that has not adequately healed and is surfacing again. In such cases, you need to try to become conscious of the wound and clean it out so it can heal.

Sometimes, depending on the nature of the wound, professional counseling can help. There may be times, however, when digging deeper into a doubt, unearthing the past surrounding the doubt, will actually make matters worse. You will now be concentrating on the doubt. The doubt will become a "project." It will seem to grow bigger the more you pay attention to it. What may have been a small shadow can turn into a looming, dark, ominous cloud. Many an insignificant doubt has turned into a full-blown marital problem because people obsessed over it and helped it grow, often with well-intentioned therapists fuelling the fire.

So, before you make matters worse by panicking at the first sign of a doubt, perhaps the first way to deal with it is the way the story suggests: just cast the doubt off; banish it to the dust.

Doubts can always enter our minds when we feel weak or tired. This is common, even in good, long-term marriages. When we realize that doubts go along with being physical, we don't have to take them so personally. We can treat them as just part of the human condition and take them more in stride. We don't have to necessarily blame ourselves for our doubts. We can just train ourselves to be conscious of them when they enter our minds and direct our free will to shoo them away. By doing so over time, we can form a positive habit to protect our minds from the snake's venom, so no damage can be done to ourselves or our marriage.

The danger with doubts is not doubts. The danger is really the self-judgment heaped upon the little weakness-of-the-flesh that a doubt is. The moment you judge yourself for a minor doubt, you have become your own serpent. You

have attacked your very soul, and shredded the fabric of
your spiritual nature. In a Garden in which you sow what
you reap, it will not be very long before the product of your
judgment against yourself will begin to appear as an event in
your life. You could actually manifest your fear as a real,
concrete event, sowing and reaping your own nightmare:

> After Rita's promotion, Michael began to feel that
> he was not the kind of husband who could keep up
> with Rita's success. He began to feel dowdy and
> "second-fiddle." After all, he was stuck home with
> wet diapers and the kids, while she was a rising star.
> Instead of shooing the doubts away, he indulged
> them. He became depressed, stopped caring about
> how he looked, gained weight, and started drink-
> ing. Over time, he actually became unattractive to
> Rita, and she began to wonder, "Is this the right
> man for me, now that I'm in the big leagues?"

Doubts, when fed, grow. But more times than not, if
you pay close attention, you will notice that you are feeding
your doubts because it is a way of caring for yourself, giving
yourself the attention and love you may badly need and
desire from your mate. Perhaps Michael would not have
felt this way about himself had he made sure to care for
himself in other ways—giving himself enough time to go
out, get his hair cut, and be good to himself personally,
without the kids in tow. Unfortunately, though, he had
picked up from his mother a bad habit of self-sacrifice for

the sake of a mate, and he was unaware of the fact that he was actually feeding his doubts subconsciously. Michael could have banished the snake had he spoken up:

> "Rita, I'm really embarrassed by the fact that you are more successful than I am. Maybe I should be working out in the world, like a normal guy?"

Rita would then have had an opportunity, as his shared soul, to help chase the snake away:

> "Honey, only a secure man like you could take care of the kids and not feel like you are less of a man. I think you are amazing."

or

> "I don't blame you for doubting yourself. I have been so self-absorbed that I haven't given you the attention you deserve. Thanks for reminding me."

Far better for Michael to receive energy from his wife than to receive energy from his own doubting self in the guise of self-criticism and blame. However, giving yourself energy through doubt is what often makes doubt an addiction that is hard to stop. Self-doubt becomes a way of giving yourself an identity and taking care of yourself when you have been ignoring yourself for the sake of others—which caused the self-doubt in the first place.

Of all the ways to counter the snake's venom, there is one that is especially difficult, but essential, especially in today's world: *stop trying to be so perfect*. In today's over-achieving environment, where Adams and Eves try to do more and accomplish more, both as individuals and as a couple, than any spouses in history, they often put enormous pressure on themselves to be perfect. They can be driven—absolutely manically driven—to achieve their perfect idea of happiness. They always seem to be hammering themselves and each other into this ideal, measuring their perfection as souls by how close they are coming to their envisioned dreams or idealistic standards.

Moreover, fed on ideal images from the media, today's Adams and Eves have a belief that there is such a thing as a perfect marriage. They create a rigid expectation for marriage, which they then judge themselves for failing to fulfill, when oftentimes their expectation was unreasonable, or even delusional, in the first place. There is no such thing as a perfect marriage. There is only a perfect spiritual process of being married that may grow more perfect as you become more aligned to perfection itself—God.

Perfection as a rigid mentally devised ideal is a notion that comes from not just any snake, but from the serpent. It is a lethal spiritual mistake, because what it says is that Adam and Eve believe that it is their idea—their finite, mental idea of perfection—that is the source of their happiness. In essence, they replace God with their own little idol, which puts them in a spiritually impossible situation: no matter what they achieve through their marriage, it will never be perfect enough, because it is not God. In setting up their mental ideal as God, today's driven Adams and Eves doom marriage after marriage, when usually nothing is really wrong except that their marriage has a certain amount of imperfection because it is human. It is their intolerance of imperfection that is the imperfection in their marriage, not the marriage itself.

In our driven world, today's Adams and Eves need to stop and give themselves a break. They need to remind themselves that it is only God who is perfection.

Take the pressure off of yourselves to be perfect or create perfection. Take the pressure off your marriage to be a perfection that it cannot be. However much you are made in the image and likeness of God, you cannot be God. However much your marriage may be heavenly, it is not *in heaven*, but on an all-too-material earth, where things can go wrong.

To doubt is to be human. To have doubts in marriage is simply part of being physical. In the order of the Garden, there will always be some "enmity" between you and the little snake. Super-natural though you both are, a few doubts are, well, just natural.

Feed those doubts, though, and they will grow into a talking serpent.

IV
THE INTIMACY BETWEEN YOU

MARRIAGE SECRET #16

Know each other's boundaries

*This one shall be called Woman
for out of Man this one was taken.
(Genesis 2:23)*

After the feminist revolution, the highly structured, rigid boundaries between men and women began to be torn down. Eve declared, in a singular voice with her sisters, "No! You're not going to overstep my boundaries, Adam. I am a distinct individual." The contemporary Adam had to learn to respect Eve's new boundaries, as well as limit his own—which wasn't easy, for male self-importance had become greatly overblown, if not destructive, over the centuries. Adam and Eve's shared soul had gotten considerably skewed on the side of Adam.

The process of developing more creative, more natural, more fluid boundaries between males and females has been going on now for decades. It is still strained, uncomfortable, and unnatural, a political and financial nightmare. Today's Adams and Eves, however freer in roles, still haven't solved the boundary problem between them as men and women. In today's Garden, they negotiate artificial boundaries like business partners, rather than as intimate mates cut from the same bolt. They draw lines, carve space, place limits, and erect "do not enter" or "traffic permitted" signs, which they each police according to their own arbitrary sense of "right" for power or privilege in the relationship—all in the name of freedom of the sexes.

Where are the true spiritual boundaries between us as mates? This is the question today's Adams and Eves are asking. If they do not discover the true boundaries between them, they will forever be victims of the next wave of political correctness. Their marriage will be based on mere convention, not God's creation.

Knowing the real boundaries between you and your mate is what the entire story of Adam and Eve was created to teach. Indeed, in the story we see all the boundaries necessary for a happy spiritual marriage put into place one at a time as the story unfolds:

First, a boundary is placed upon the original human, separating male and female. This boundary says, "You are separate souls, but a shared soul. In your marriage you must not act for yourself alone, but must consider the other."

Second, a boundary is placed between Adam and Eve and the Tree of Knowledge. This boundary says, "You are not the source of knowledge, even if you eat a bite of knowledge. No matter what you know, stop substituting your idea of order in marriage for God's order. You're not in charge."

Third, after overstepping their boundaries with their private desires, Adam and Eve place a boundary of fig leaves on their "private parts." This boundary says, "You must always make yourselves conscious of your own inner life and motivations, and not manipulate your unsuspecting mate for your own psychological issues or desires."

Fourth, God gives Adam and Eve a difficult, painful reminder of all the boundaries they have violated, binding them, and the serpent, into their right place. This boundary says, "If you don't learn boundaries in marriage the easy way, you'll learn them the hard way—but, you'll learn them. You can't escape the order of the universe. How much suffering you experience in your marriage is up to you; the less you respect God's boundaries, the more pain you will experience."

Fifth, social boundaries, on male and female behaviors, patterned largely on "animal natures," come into play. This boundary says, "Cooperate. You have a mutual task to support yourselves and create life. Your behaviors must be harmonious and compatible for the shared task of marriage, which touches upon society, the entire world, and everything in existence. The whole universe depends on the boundaries between you."

Sixth, the definitive finite boundary of "animal skins" or a physical body is placed upon their naked souls as a covering for protection. This boundary says, "You can't escape until you learn the lesson of boundaries. It is a lesson built into your flesh."

At each successive stage, the boundary gets more and more dense, until, by the sixth boundary, Adam and Eve are literally sealed within the boundaries of God's creation. The essential boundaries of God's order are formed into their flesh, which they must inhabit and learn about. Adam and Eve will learn about creation's boundaries as they learn about their bodies' boundaries—by reproducing, propagating life, building a shared life and human civilization together. Their own physical bodies are God's basic lesson in boundaries after their fall into the physical—or their elevation to being co-creators with free will; depending on one's religious point of view, it's an original sin or an original gift.

So, the answer to the question that plagues today's Adams and Eves—Where are the true spiritual boundaries between us as mates?—is surprisingly simple:

Your real boundaries are right there, alive and breathing as your actual physical bodies, and these boundaries include all the boundaries in God's creation.

Up until now, we've spoken of boundaries from an intellectual viewpoint for the purpose of distinguishing all the different levels of creation to which a spiritual marriage must align. But such a view of boundaries is one-sided and can become lopsided without another view of boundaries—a far more important view—boundaries based on *feeling*. Like male and female, left brain and right brain, a clear-cut, intelligently understood boundary between today's Adams and Eves must merge with intuition, a sixth sense, an instinct—a *feeling-understanding* about right and proper boundaries between you.

There is a tone, a manner, a feeling, a nuance, a grace, and a dance to right, proper, respectful, and safe boundaries between married partners. It is never just black or white, right or wrong. There is a beauty to the boundaries between partners, a subtle body-language to it. God's boundaries are not just a simple austere rational order, but form a super-rational (beyond mental) order that is completely and fully integrated with feeling on all scales of existence—from the tiniest order of the atom to the mega-order of our universe, and perhaps universes beyond. It is impossible to intellectually fathom all the details of true spiritual boundaries. However, they can be fathomed through feeling.

Feeling connects you to God's intention for creation and, therefore, to all the boundaries in existence, simultaneously. There's no better teacher for feelings than your body. That's why God put you in one—to make you more aware of the impulses of your soul by translating them into powerful bodily feelings, so you can more easily learn about yourself.

Your body is a giant feeling-machine. All the feelings in creation—the indescribable spiritual forces that weave sense, sensation, texture and tone, pleasure and pain, love and hate throughout the universe—all the infinitely complex feeling-boundaries in cosmic life are woven in and through your body. Before they are even consciously acknowledged as emotions or thought, they are felt first in your body as sensations. Only by tuning in to feeling can today's marriages—scripted with pre-nuptial agreements, palimony, and childrearing contracts—which are every bit as rigid as in the past—be restored to flowing, joyful spiritual experiences between men and women: innocence reborn in the Garden.

Your bodies express the experiences of your soul. They amplify the impulses of your soul, so you can become conscious of your soul-nature through feeling. Thus, to be aware of the feeling-signals of your body is to become more conscious of your soul. Pay attention in different situations to how your body feels and how you feel in your body, and you will learn virtually all you need to know about right and proper boundaries between you. Here are some of the most obvious boundaries that bodily feeling can teach you:

Push your mate to the point of pain, emotionally and physically, and it feels bad. God has placed a boundary upon you, to teach you to not cause needless hurt.

Violate the feelings of your mate, and he will experience a feeling of constriction, rigidity, and even fear in his body. God has placed a boundary upon you, to teach you to not be cruel.

Goad your partner past her physical and emotional limits, and it causes increased heart rate, anxiety, and stress. God has placed a boundary upon you, to teach you to not disregard the health of your mate.

Embarrass your spouse and his body reacts immediately with flushing or blanching; his blood pressure will plummet or rise. God has placed a boundary upon you, to teach you never to embarrass your partner.

Impose yourself upon your mate, insisting that your feelings are more important than her feelings, and her soul's boundaries will suffer; she'll experience shortness of breath, an inability to speak, a

constriction in her throat. God has placed a boundary upon you, so you learn never to overstep your
bounds.

There are many such boundaries that your body's
feeling-sense can teach you about. Your "animal skin" is
truly a covering that acts as protection for your soul. The
more you tune into the feelings of your body, the more you
will naturally learn about the right and proper boundaries
between you and your mate. In general, it is only when
spouses avoid feeling feelings that they overstep the natural
spiritual boundaries of creation and cause banishment for
themselves and their mates.

However, you don't have to spend a lifetime monitoring your feelings, living on the inside rather than enjoying
life on the outside. Nor, despite what many of today's
Adams and Eves think, do you need to turn your marriage
into a sterile classroom or a group therapy session in order
to establish right and correct boundaries. There is one
boundary that is the origin of all these boundaries, one
feeling that is the origin of all these instructive feelings:
God's love.

Master God's love and you'll master all the boundaries!

God's love set the boundaries on creation. It was God's
love that said "Don't" to Adam and Eve.

God's love is the substance of our physical feelings.
God's love forms the fleshly feeling-boundaries that surround our souls. Our souls are God's own love boundaried
in us.

God's love is the only boundary that needs to grow between you. Your feelings of love need to grow more and more until they reflect God's love and approach the full expression of God's love.

Master the boundary of all boundaries, God's love, and all the other little boundaries—rational or emotional—will fall right into place.

MARRIAGE SECRET #17

Practice naked honesty

Then the eyes of both were opened,
and they knew that they were naked;
and they sewed fig leaves together
and made loincloths for themselves.
(Genesis 3:7)

Now that right and proper boundaries are established between you, you can feel safe enough to take a major spiritual leap together as a couple: you are ready to stop lying to each other.

Lying is the single biggest cause—if not the *only* cause—of problems between spouses. One spouse lies to the other and therefore sows a lie in the marriage. The other spouse then reacts to the lie, unconsciously or consciously altering his behavior and actions. This then intensifies the lie, so now you have two people sowing a lie, which plants the lie deeper into the soil of the Garden. Before you know it, one person's lie, now two persons' lie, materializes in their shared lives as a full-blown event. They have reaped the fruit of their lie as a concrete experience in the Garden.

Not surprisingly, the fruit of these experiences tastes terrible to both of them. God presents them with their lies, clothed as their problems. But, rather than stopping and realizing that God has simply given them what they asked for through the lies they sowed, Adam and Eve often cover up their lies with yet another lie, which then sows another level of lies, covering up the previous lie. Round after round of lying takes place, until marriages can literally become buried under a mountain of lies. Separation and divorce become the only apparent way to cut through the lies and wipe the slate clean. However, after the divorce, the previous spouse, now a new spouse, doesn't stop lying, and the process begins all over again with a different spouse. Divorces will never end until lies end.

Here are three common lies spouses tell each other:

Certainly I'll do it, if it makes you happy. This sounds like nobility and generosity of heart. However, in many cases the speaker has learned and is repeating a dangerous lie called, "It is noble to sacrifice oneself for another." Self-sacrifice is noble for a higher cause, or when lives are at stake; it is masochistic otherwise. This lie makes the receiver happy and the giver miserable.

I consider it my responsibility to work as hard as I can to support you. There is truth here, but the lie that remains unspoken is: "Feel indebted to me. Adore me. Allow me to make all the important decisions by myself, because I am so good to you." Such magnanimous providers often work themselves sick and make others feel guilty for it.

Let's talk about this before you go ahead with it. This lie is so pervasive that it's virtually a sitcom. What's really being said is: "I totally disagree with you. What you are planning will wreck my life, and you don't know it yet, but you are *not* going ahead with it." This is hardly a spiritual helpmate at work. "Let's talk" denotes an "us," but the lie here is that this will be a monologue, not a dialogue.

Lies can be partial truths. Lies can be overstatements of truth. Lies can be withholding of truth.

Lies can also be false beliefs. We may actually think they are true, because we see other people living a certain way and want to believe that's "the truth." Many of today's Adams and Eves have lied to themselves: "All we want is a nice house in the suburbs with a family and a dog." One side of them may want this because they are seeking parental approval, perhaps because they were overly wild and crazy when they were single and are now making amends. However, they are often lying to another side of themselves that wants nothing at all of what their parents had and wishes to live as far away from a rut as possible, but is afraid of disapproval.

Soon their lie results in their dream house. Gradually, the lie drains their youth, their enthusiasm, their money, their dreams, and their individuality. They feel closed in and start to fight. Before you know it, they separate and meet someone who makes them feel young again.

Indeed, if you look at virtually everything that goes wrong with your dreams, you will discover, if you're honest, that the problem is rooted in some kind of false belief. You are lying to yourself to please another, or following someone else's truth as your own, which is *always* a lie.

Most of the time, lies are unintentional. We aren't fully aware of what we are doing, any more than the biblical couple was:

> We lie because we fear rejection by our spouse if we were to say what we really feel.

> We lie because we wish to control our spouse, even through falsity, because we have given away our free will, something we should not have done.

> We lie because we mistrust our mates and think we must lie to protect ourselves.

> We lie because we do not believe that life or people are actually good, and we think we must manipulate

others to feel safe and supported, rather than relying on the grace in the Garden to provide for us.

But all these reasons are just disguises for the deeper reason for lying: we don't trust ourselves. We have gotten lost in
the serpentine webs of our own mind, doubting the voice of
God within our own soul. We have stopped trusting the
voice of our true self and have substituted a false voice, the
serpent's voice, for our own God-given conscience.

Trust yourself and you won't have to lie to your mate
or to anyone else. Trust yourself and you'll experience your
natural connection to God's grace; God's life flows through
you as confidence in your own life. Trust yourselves, and
your shared-soul relationship will be reestablished on the
truth of God's Being. You can then strip off your defense
mechanisms, the fig leaves that protect you from your
innocence, and practice one of the most powerful tools for
creating a spiritual marriage: naked honesty.

Naked honesty means that you feel so safe with your
mate that you are absolutely free to be, do, and say what
you really feel, without any second thoughts. You can
express yourself totally, secure in your physical boundaries,
experiencing only feelings of comfort and delight while
doing so. Naked honesty means you can be a soul in a body,
but no less a soul—living in truth, living as truth, living the
truth of God's Being, which you are, individualized in
human form.

Naked honesty also means that you are capable of creating that kind of naked safety for your mate. It means that

even if you hear something you may disagree with, your body doesn't clinch, your eyes don't narrow, your skin doesn't flush. You show none of the boundary signs that indicate you are disapproving of your mate's honesty. Naked honesty means total openness to the movement of the other person's soul, and so it requires total openness to the movement of your own soul. It means maintaining your separateness as individuals, but consciously permitting yourself to *feel* the other person, thereby creating a shared-soul boundary together. You actually permit the other person to speak into your soul, and you can speak honestly into your partner's soul. You allow your mate's words to resonate within you, reverberating off the cords of your heart, and hear the music she is playing to you. Such a melody will always communicate your mate's inner truth, and yours as well.

Naked honesty is so intimate that it cannot be practiced nonchalantly. Today's Adams and Eves often confuse naked honesty with bluntness. They crudely blurt out what they think without any regard for their tone and manner, justifying themselves by saying, "I'm just being honest." This is not naked honesty. This kind of "honesty" is clothed in deceit. Some aspect of one spouse is being threatened by the other spouse, and that threat is being covered up by a willfulness that is crude, even violent-sounding, in an attempt to control the other.

True naked honesty is not that. It's as innocent as a breeze through a window. It's not affected or disguised. You can tell when the honesty is naked, because:

You feel no stress in your body, no discomfort in the pit of your stomach.

Eye contact can be maintained without effort.

Your tone of voice stays considerate and you are aware of its effect on the other person.

There is a soul-sense, a kind of "holiness" to the air of the conversation, a spiritual warmth.

There are moments of silence, because each spouse is truly listening on a soul-level, taking in what the other spouse is saying.

You aren't stepping on each other's words to get in what you think.

As naked honesty continues to develop, it can go beyond words and body language. You can actually begin to feel so safe that you can relinquish your personal boundaries. You can mutually penetrate past each other's psychic fig leaves and feel your souls come together in a shared-soul boundary. You can actually begin to feel the truth of each other as pieces of God. Another word for this level of naked honesty could be said to be "communion." You commune with the soul of your mate in a manner similar to the way you would commune with the ultimate soul, which is God.

When this kind of naked honesty is achieved, two souls come together at one level of spiritual awareness, but when they separate from their communion, they will have moved to a higher level. Somehow—although you may not be able to fully understand what has taken place, because it has occurred below the level of your conscious mind—you will sense a kind of transfiguring effect from the experience of naked honesty. You may go off on your way, do the things you need to do, and continue with life as usual, but it will not be long before you will notice that something in you has changed, and that in subsequent interactions with other people, in subsequent tasks you may need to perform, you are acting differently. It's as if spiritual knowledge has been "downloaded" into you through your mate. Indeed, it has. In naked honesty that reaches the point of communion, the two soul-halves come together and exchange knowledge, not just in the form of words, but in the form of spirit, invigorating each other and bringing each other closer to completeness. You actually pick up a higher spiritual energy or "dose" of grace from God, which you transmit to each other, raising you both to a greater level of conscious awareness of God.

So, naked honesty, although it begins with not lying to yourself or to your mate, goes considerably deeper, returning you to the original consciousness from which Adam and Eve departed when they began their experience of physicality.

One would think that naked honesty was something the biblical couple should have known instinctually, since they were so freshly separated from their original soul. However, *too* freshly separated, they needed to first learn the boundaries of their individualities. Naked honesty requires strong

egos, sturdy spiritual legs, clear-mindedness, and an unshak-
able individuality that no one can dilute. It is only when you
are fully anchored in your soul that you can feel safe enough
to lose your fig leaves and re-merge with your mate in a
deeper, more intimate communion.

Naked honesty, therefore, takes practice. It is not something that can be achieved instantly, and there is nothing
wrong with you if you find that the level of naked honesty
you can currently achieve is less than perfect. There is no
measuring-rod here, no standard that anyone can impose
upon you. It is an intuitive sense between you and your
partner of knowing where the blocks are, where the disguised truths are, where the hidden or overt lies are and
consciously deciding to direct your wills past them to a
greater, more open nakedness of souls between you.

Other than the lessons uncovered in our discussion of the
previous fourteen marriage secrets, there are no tips on how
to approach naked honesty. You will experience ups and
downs, huge road blocks, or just tiny nuances of the other
person's lack of honesty or of your own: an odd turn of a
smile, a flick of an eyebrow. These may reflect minor insecu-
rities or they may be superficial signs of a deeper, spiritual
insecurity that is hidden. Regardless, they are indications of
clothed honesty that needs to be stripped bare.

Once you make the shared commitment to embark on
naked honesty, God will guide you. Step by step, you will
feel yourselves being led down a path to remove the fig
leaves that separate you as souls. Each leaf drops, followed
by the next leaf, and the next, in an orderly fashion linked

to God's own truth-process, happening exactly at the correct pace for both of your souls. It's an astonishing experience of shared providence between you, remarkable, even breathtaking. That's because making a commitment to naked honesty is making a faith-commitment to each other and God simultaneously. It is the ultimate pledge of your forthrightness and sincere desire to align with the order of creation and enter into a spiritual marriage. When you do that, the higher power behind all life supports you and nurtures you on the path.

The purpose of life in the Garden is to grow toward truth. The purpose is not just the satisfaction of your material desires, dreams, or adventures—a "nice, comfortable marriage." If you concentrate merely on the outward things, you can achieve them, sowing and reaping more delights than you can handle in a lifetime. But you may become so blinded that you may miss out on the true inner purpose of a shared relationship: the spiritual achievement of nakedly honest truth, the experience of God's truth being exchanged and growing between you.

The lie is always putting "the world" before God, the serpent before the Lord, the created before the Creator. Build your life on naked honesty and you'll build your marriage on the rock of truth.

MARRIAGE SECRET #18

Turn away from temptation

*For God knows that when you eat of it your eyes will be opened,
and you will be like God, knowing good and evil.
(Genesis 3:5)*

Now that you have mastered naked honesty, what better time to discuss the most nakedly *dis*-honest thing that can ever happen to a marriage: infidelity—or, as it is commonly and correctly called, cheating.

When you cheat on your mate, you are cheating on all life in the Garden. First, cheating cheats the shared soul of which you are both parts. When you cheat on your mate's soul, you cheat on your own soul simultaneously. You violate the pieces of God you are, and therefore God. Second, cheating cheats the divine truth that forms the fabric of all reality. It's a dishonesty that works havoc with the order of truth upon which all life and existence are founded. Third, cheating violates society. Marital vows are public, made in the presence of family, friends, and associates. Cheating violates the love between others and you, as much as between you as mates. Fourth, cheating cheats all humanity, because marriage is the cornerstone of all human relationships and each marriage must, by virtue of its total dependency, touch upon everyone in God's Garden. Fifth, cheating cheats all future generations, since it undermines the respect between parents and children, preventing the growth of truth, knowledge, and love from generation to generation; the very process of divine creativity is undermined by cheating. Sixth, cheating cheats our very planet, because it is the misuse of our bodies (a part of nature), as we shall discuss in more detail in the next chapter.

Cheating is cheating everything and everyone in existence. It is not—ever—insignificant or "just a fling."

Today's Adams and Eves have all sorts of very ingenious explanations for why couples cheat on each other:

> Wandering eyes
>
> Not having finished adolescence
>
> Sexual dissatisfaction
>
> Poor role models
>
> The need to express oneself
>
> The inability to control one's urges
>
> Rebellion against control by one's mate

A leftover from the "sixties"

Feeling closed-in in marriage

Not having grown up

"That's just men"

Sexual liberation

The need to experiment

There is a certain amount of truth to all these things. However, underneath them all, there is only one real explanation for why couples cheat: they cannot face themselves and they cannot face the other. One or both are hiding from themselves, from the other, from God, and from creation, as did the biblical couple.

This is not to say that there are no grounds for marital dissatisfaction, and that such marital dissatisfaction cannot lead to succumbing to temptation. Alas, the flesh is as tempting as Eve's apple. However, the bottom line is that cheating—done for whatever reason, whether seemingly justifiable or unjustifiable—is simply a *lie*. One spouse in a relationship has chosen to violate the trust, honesty, and soul-connection between himself and his spouse, on his own initiative, without consulting or considering his spouse. He has taken upon himself the right to simply do what he wishes, in a universe in which individual freedom must be married to responsibility toward God's order. In essence, the reason for all cheating is simply the reason for Adam and Eve's fall: making your own self so important that it excludes your marriage and the marriage between you and all existence, asserting your individuality in a way that is not aligned to all the orders of existence. That is, of course, why cheating is considered a sin.

Cheating usually occurs because, for some reason, you are so overwhelmed by your feelings that you "don't know what's come over" you. The serpent lures you in to the point that you forget your conscious commitment to each other and God's order, as did the biblical couple. The impulse of your emotions becomes so much stronger than your rational mind that reason dims and your feelings inundate you. The flood of urges that follows drowns your better instincts. Therefore, cheating is caused not just by a simple feeling, but by feelings that have become danger-ously powerful, emotions that have become overcharged, ready to release a lightning bolt that can decimate every-thing you've worked so hard to achieve together.

How does such a storm get started? Generally speak-ing, with repression.

Most couples think that in order to prevent themselves from cheating they must repress themselves. They must avert their lustful eyes; they must bury their attraction to other people; they must close themselves off, place their feel-ings in a box, and seal their emotions in a can—hermetically, like a hermit.

A certain amount of repression is necessary, because it is part of keeping your attention on your commitment to the marriage. It's a way of not letting stray feelings sidetrack you, of not indulging in "cheating by thought." Unchecked, these tiny "mental interludes" can build force and actually sow and reap infidelity in the flesh.

However, when such negative repression becomes excessive—a fearful obsession to eliminate every glance at someone you may find attractive—it can reach a limit, creating something like a cement wall around natural human emotion and sexuality. Cement always cracks when it has no sway, which is why sidewalks are made in sections to allow for breathing room. With excess negative repression, there is no breathing room. Rather than preventing infidelity, such repression can actually contribute to causing it.

The lack of breathing room in marriage is caused by emotions that one or the other spouse has learned to consider "not right" or unacceptable and therefore is holding in or holding back. She may have learned this behavior from societal norms, excessively stringent religious rules, or cultural ideals, or she may have inherited parental inhibitions or psychological problems, especially guilt. The effect may be reinforced by the personality of her mate, who may have had similar programming.

When normal emotions are overly repressed, they can grow in force until a terrible tension, even antagonism, develops between mind and feelings. This can disturb a spouse's peace of mind, and when the problem is projected outside the relationship to an "attraction," it can disrupt the marriage. If one spouse happens to add his repression to the repression the other carries inside, then even more pressure can be put on both spouses to repress their feelings. Such a marriage can literally repress itself into extinction, or an explosion. On the other hand, if the other spouse happens to be freer and wants his mate to not be so repressed, then he can put pressure on his mate to *de*-repress. The emotions underneath the repression may be so threatening that they actually cause even greater stress. Such a couple might literally open a can of worms for which they are largely unprepared.

Negative repression is a "Catch-22" that usually requires professional counseling to work through. It is a keg of dynamite waiting to be lit by one moment of weakness. Such weakness is really just a chink in the armor of someone who has become overly armored to protect herself from natural feelings she has learned to consider "wrong." It's over-repression that has made these feelings unnaturally explosive.

If you engage in negative repression, there are usually some very telling signs. When temptation appears...

You just cannot stop "thinking about it."

As you try to stomp on repeated fantasies, their fire burns hotter. They take over your mental life, your emotional life, your business and personal life.

Inwardly, you may feel emotionally dead or frozen, because you are also not permitting ordinary natural feelings, while you are repressing "unnatural" ones.

You are overly intellectual, or distant, because you have jumped into your head in order to distance yourself from your feelings of guilt.

Be honest with yourself. If you recognize these signs in yourself, first, be honest with your mate, tell him what you are feeling, and seek his help. It often happens that when you begin to be honest about your feelings, they begin to dissipate, especially when you realize your spouse loves and accepts you for who you are, "good" or "bad." If you learned such repression from parents who were overly conditional in the way they loved you, unconditional love from a spouse may be just the antidote you need.

However, this may not be enough. Indeed, such negative repression may be a symptom not just of one spouse's problems, but also of a shared problem that neither of you may be conscious of. In either case, do not assign blame, ever.

Feelings—even excessive ones—are human. As in all experiences in God's Garden, use this as an opportunity to grow spiritually closer and more open. Allow your feelings to surface as a spiritual challenge that can, if you both face the challenge together, bring your marriage closer.

After all, not all repression is negative. Some repression is actually quite positive, and can be the foundation for a healthy monogamous marriage, one in which cheating is off-limits, but there is no cement wall needed to contain it. Such positive repression is an art that is well worth learning.

Let's suppose that you or your spouse notices someone, repeatedly, who is attracting you emotionally and sexually, and you just can't stop looking. You may notice your heart beating faster when you see that person; you may notice yourself creating all sorts of manipulative ways you conjure up to meet or speak to the person, even when there is a side of you that knows you are opening the door to temptation. With positive repression, you do not blame yourself, beat yourself up, or flagellate your feelings. They are, after all, your feelings, a part of you, and you should honor them. Instead, you allow yourself to be human. You ever-so-gently separate from these feelings and stand back from them, observing yourself lovingly, perhaps with a good sense of humor:

"Look at me. You'd swear I was back in school again. Well, it's nice to know I still can feel like a teenager. But—I love my spouse and I've made a commitment; so, I'm not touching this apple, no matter how tempting it looks."

This is the kind of self-awareness that the newly created Adam and Eve were unable to muster. This kind of positive repression gives you a moment of clarity in which to order your priorities and not allow your impulses to undermine the order of your lives and your spiritual commitment to each other. This kind of positive repression also short-circuits shame. Shame is what the biblical couple experienced after succumbing to temptation. Shame can cause chronic guilt, like a dark, clinging cloud that hangs around long after the temptation has passed. Positive repression can help inject some light into that, and prevent the cloud from forming.

With positive repression, you do not deny your feelings. You accept your feelings with love. By applying love to your problem, you protect yourself from losing yourself and your marriage. With positive repression, you "love yourself into line." This draws God's protection down to you, because God's essence is love. You become quickly centered, both emotionally and mentally. In essence, because you have asked for help, a strengthening of your alignment to God's order, you will receive that help. God's protection comes the moment it is asked for, which is why positive repression is much more powerful than negative repression. It is aligned through love to the order of creation, rather than being based upon self-criticism, self-punishment, and condemnation.

However, even after applying positive repression, you may still feel a little hollow. After all, infidelity—even in thought—can rip through your soul and make you question your spiritual integrity. You may not know what to do with all those feelings and wonder why your full devotion and attention are not being given to your other half, especially if you are truly spiritually committed to each other:

"Why am I looking?"

"What is missing?"

"What is this saying about me, or my spouse?"

Even though positive repression is more powerful than negative, and is the preferred spiritual technique for avoiding temptation, your conscience can still be left aching. That's why repression, in any form, is just the beginning. The most advanced and most spiritually blessed way of turning away from temptation is what I call "divine suppression."

Suppression is not repression. It doesn't "just say no" and walk away from the feelings. Suppression takes those hanging emotions surrounding an act of infidelity, either in the flesh or in the mind, and uses them constructively. It is *sup*-pression, a pressing under—a placing of the pressure you are feeling under God's order for the heightening of your spiritual purpose.

With divine suppression, you think about all the qualities that the person who is attracting you has—looks, personality, body—all the things that are luring you in. Then, you use each of these qualities as tools to draw you closer to your soul, your mate's soul, and God. You actually use your temptation as a gift to expand your soul. You begin by asking yourself:

In what way do I wish I had those qualities I'm attracted to?

Could my attraction for that other person be an indication of something missing in me?

If in honest reflection this is the case, through divine suppression you make a decision to develop those qualities in yourself. If you find the person intelligent, you work to improve your own intelligence; if you find the person's positive attitude attractive, you make a commitment to develop your own sense of optimism. Satisfying that hunger within you will suppress your hunger for the other person.

Next, ask yourself these questions:

In what way do I wish my mate had those qualities?

In what way is this attraction an indication of something my mate is not providing for me?

With divine suppression, you speak to your mate about what you find attractive and what qualities you wish she possessed. Because you are bound in total dependency, your mate should be willing to look at himself and develop that trait as an act of giving. If you are attracted to someone slimmer, perhaps it's time your mate lost weight. If you are attracted to someone who is perhaps more polite, your mate may need to perfect his manners when he is around you. (Having been born in Brooklyn, my personal politeness needs quite a lot of work.) Such an honest communication with your mate could turn out to be exactly what your mate needs to know about himself, and your temptation may be turned into a gift to him. It is not necessary to actually mention the temptation-incident itself—unless it is a chronic problem. It is just necessary to talk, in general, about what you find attractive and desirous that you'd like your mate to emulate. You do not want to encourage your spouse to think that there is a serious infidelity problem when there is just a mere momentary temptation.

In virtually all cases of temptation, you are projecting onto the object of desire some quality that is missing either in yourself or in your mate and, therefore, in your shared soul. Divine suppression gives you the opportunity to take these qualities, become aware of them, and fold them back into your marriage. The spiritual energy you might lose through an unfaithful glance or fantasy becomes recycled to energize your marriage and your shared life. Making a habit of divine suppression can actually strengthen your marriage and continually revitalize it, making it virtually impervious to a temptation that could undermine or destroy it. Why? Because with divine suppression infidelity actually becomes a tool for strengthening fidelity. You convert potential sin into a blessing, and so your marriage is actually empowered. You turn from the serpent toward God.

However, sometimes you may also discover, upon reflection, that there is nothing either in you or your mate that you are projecting upon the object of desire. You are just plain attracted, for no apparent reason. In this case, divine suppression means offering the event to God as an opportunity for learning and expanding spiritually. You say prayerfully:

"Oh, well, I don't know why I'm attracted to this person. But, it's not part of my vow to my mate, or to God and creation, so I'm returning this event to the universe, and releasing it for the purpose of

God's goodness. In exchange, give me knowledge
that can improve my relationship with my mate
and creation's order."

This prayer releases the hidden power of your soul, a
power that can help you deal with the challenge of temptation. If you stay alert to how God's Garden operates, you
will soon notice some curious event or occurrence taking
place in your life. As you think about it, you will begin to
understand more fully what that previous attraction was all
about. For instance, you may eventually realize that the
person resembles an old flame from the past, someone with
whom you didn't break up amicably. It may be that your
attraction was actually a message from God that it is time
to forgive and release your resentment, and the attraction
was not really an act of temptation as such. It is amazing,
but often even the most insignificant attractions have very
deep meanings. Nothing happens by chance. Even the
hairs on our heads are numbered.

But, remember, don't be too hard on yourself. There is a
rarely a spouse in any marriage that has never been attracted
to someone else. Our natures as single people don't just die
when we tie the knot. However, it is up to us to constantly
realign our single natures to our marital commitment, so
that they work harmoniously in a shared-soul relationship.
More often than not, momentary attractions are usually
signs that your shared souls have separated from their
shared spiritual purpose and that some gentle adjustment is
needed.

If you've been working on dynamically balancing freedom, oneness, and goodness in your marriage—so that no
one feels "closed in"—and you've been learning the lessons
of the marriage secrets we've been discussing, committing
yourselves to a life of shared spiritual growth, chances are
that temptations, even if they do come, will not be quite so
tempting. You will not need to think about whether they
should be negatively repressed, positively repressed, or
divinely suppressed. You will simply flick temptations off
like mosquitoes, knowing that the more you let them
linger, the more they will draw blood. You will nip temptation in the bud—on the level of thought—before it sows
and reaps a fleshly act of outright marital infidelity.

If that's the case, congratulate yourself. The snake may
have nipped at your heel, but you have bruised its head, as
God told a fleshly Adam and Eve to do.

The heel is the back part of the foot, the past. If you
take a step toward temptation, put it behind you fast, and
neither one of you will ever get hurt.

MARRIAGE SECRET #19

Your bodies are not just your own

And the man and his wife were both naked,
and were not ashamed.
(Genesis 2:25)

Today's Adams and Eves tend to believe that they own their own bodies. They consider their bodies "theirs"—to do with as they please, whenever and however they want. They feel free to walk, run, and pump iron. They feel free to dress the way they want. They feel free to eat whatever foods they want. And they often feel free to sleep with whomever they wish, use their bodies in any way they choose, and indulge any sexual activity that comes to mind. Why? Because they believe that their bodies are exclusively theirs, and they are free to do as they wish with them.

They *are* free. All of us are granted the freedom by God to use our bodies as we desire. However, this does not mean that such freedom comes without consequences, that there are no limits to that freedom. Today's Adams and Eves often think they live in some abstract universe that has no order to it. You may eat sugary and fatty foods. That is your right, because you have been given the gift of freedom. However, God has designed your body in such a way that there are consequences, such as coronary occlusion, diabetes, and a host of other maladies if you over-indulge. You may choose to sleep with anyone you want and explore every imaginable sexual pleasure. However, God has designed creation in a way that does not seem to tolerate sexual extremes. After any period when promiscuous behavior has become excessive, a period of venereal disease often follows to stem the excessiveness and restore a natural balance. This happened in the roaring twenties, with syphilis; it happened in the rip-roaring seventies, eighties, and nineties with herpes and now AIDS.

Although your body is yours, there are consequences when you use your freedom in a way that is not consonant with the order of creation. Therefore, your body is not just your property. It is not a house you "own." It is really more of a rental property, leased to you by God, and if you vandalize the property, the owner holds you accountable.

The entire order of creation—from the level of the cosmos to the level of the human cell, from sub-cellular organelles to subatomic structures, from subatomic structures to pure energy—is organized in a very detailed and personal way to create what we all fliply call "*my* body."

Your body is the actual body of the universe that you inhabit. Your body is, more specifically, the planet Earth, and all its complex ecological systems, embodied in human form. How you treat or use your body affects all life and all nature on our planet. If you abuse your body, you are abusing the body of creation and undermining God's intention for it. If you abuse the body of another person, you are also abusing the body of creation and undermining God's intention for it. Since your body and the body of creation are not separate, if you abuse another person's body, you are simultaneously abusing your own body; the effects of your actions are simultaneously visited upon you.

Yes, indeed, there is a moral order to the proper use of the body. If some spiritual authorities in the past were overly strident, overly controlling and inhuman with regard to the body, advocating its repression, denying its goodness, refusing its desires, it's also true that movements that sought to counteract this excess created their own excess in the process: lack of discretion, wantonness, and libertine behavior. Sometimes, this went as far as outright degeneracy— acting against the generating process of creation, God's own creativity.

There is a moral order to the proper use of your body, not because God is standing up in heaven with a ruler, ready to rap your knuckles if you have an evil thought or a creative fantasy. God is neither a prude nor an exhibitionist; these are human projections. There is a moral order because it is God's design, inescapably built into the very nature of creation. There are simply laws of creation to which every body (everybody's body) must align itself. With the lease of a body comes big-time responsibility, because you are utilizing a precious piece of real estate: God's creation. Your capacity to interfere with God's intention for the human species, and all of life, is powerful. We all suffer when your body, or any body, is not aligned to God's order.

Your body *is* God's order, as it is expressed on the plane of physical life. You are literally clothed in God's order. Indeed, that was what the "punishment" of Adam and Eve was about. Once they had bitten off a piece of knowledge and discovered their divine ability as co-creators, God clothed them in the Garden's order so they would learn about it. God's order, which is built into their physical bodies, instructs their souls in the laws of the Garden. As Adam and Eve learn more about themselves as physical beings, they learn more about God's physical creation, the Garden around them.

Needless to say, the enormous responsibility that goes with having a body affects human beings most intimately in marriage, which, physically, is the actual union of two bodies. In a marriage, the universal moral laws surrounding the body come into play in the most personal of ways—in the bedroom. Right and proper alignment of your body and the body of your mate to each other and the entire body of creation is a spiritual imperative for marriage. It also creates many of the complexities and difficulties of married life. Even when a couple is not aware of it, there are often tugs and pulls by forces seemingly bigger than they, forces of nature that live within their bodies. Many of these forces account for the sparring and outright competition between mates in the course of their marriage. These are animal-like drives—subtle, and often unconscious—that spouses cannot fully master until they fully spiritualize their lives. As we all know, it is not at all uncommon to feel your body's desire move in one direction, your heart's desire in another direction, and your mind's desire in yet another direction. If this kind of confusion happens in just one indi-vidual, it doubles in a marriage.

Much of the confusion can end, though, when spouses develop a right and proper relationship with their bodies. Your body is God's anchor. When it is properly aligned to God's creation, properly aligned to your mate, then the other aspects of your spiritual nature, such as your heart and your mind, come into line more easily. Your soul is planted firmly on the ground, which, of course, is the very purpose of your body in the first place.

Spiritually guiding your bodies into alignment with each other and creation is a complex art—far too complex to handle in detail in this chapter; it would require another book to do it justice. However, there are a few basics, a few dos and don'ts that might be of help. They pertain to all aspects of physical life—eating, home-making, work, and play. But, they are most critical when it comes to the direct merging of two bodies in sexuality:

Seek balance. Extremes are natural when they are momentary passions as part of a sustained, organic, balance. Extremes are like salt and pepper, spices that enhance the flavor but are never the main course. Bodies, and relationships, blossom with balance.

That which is pleasurable is good for you, provided it is simultaneously good for your mate, your family, and God's order. Never mistake good for just what feels good or what you believe is good.

That which is not pleasurable is generally bad for you. There are natural foods, natural desires that just feel right. Listen to God's voice through your pleasure or lack of pleasure. If you don't like something, it is generally something you should avoid.

Pleasure is not an end in itself. Pleasure is the gift of God when you satisfy the spiritual purpose of life in the body. Eating divinely, sleeping divinely, making love divinely all produce pleasure as a reward. Pleasure should be a consequence—a result —of the godly use of your body.

Never violate your body's health except in life-and-death situations. Only if life is at stake and you need to push your body way beyond itself, perhaps to save someone else, should you ever risk your own physical body. Be careful about martyrdom for money, for love, for pleasures. You don't want to undermine the most precious gift of all: health, physical and spiritual.

Trust the voice of your conscience. Your body has an inner sense of what aligns it to God's order and what doesn't. You can hear its voice through your conscience; your conscience connects you to God. However, always remember to inform your conscience by listening to other voices too: your physician's, society's, your mate's, your faith's. This can help keep you from thinking that your conscience exists in isolation, that it is simply the expression of "what I want to do and the hell with you."

The last—and perhaps the most basic—truth about the body, the one that sums up all of them, indeed, the basic of all basics:

Your body serves God first, creation second, you third, and your mate fourth. This order is sacred.

First, the purpose of your body is to serve as a vehicle for spiritual expansion. Second, the purpose of your body is to serve as a vehicle by which creation grows and expands in a life-giving balance of freedom, oneness, and goodness that includes family life, society, and all life on the planet.

Third, the purpose of your body is to serve your needs personally, including your own personal pleasures. And fourth, the purpose of your body is also to serve your mate's needs and personal pleasures.

This last purpose—the purpose of your body in terms of your mate's pleasure—is a very delicate matter, especially today when many women have "taken their bodies back" from men because of abuse in the past. In a spiritual marriage, one that seeks to align you and your mate to creation, your body can never be "taken back" from men; nor, for that matter, can men ever "take back" their bodies from women. If your bodies are not just your own in terms of the entire order of creation, this is certainly even more so in a monogamous marriage, where spouses have made themselves exclusively dependent upon each other for the satisfaction of their bodily desires.

In a shared-soul marriage, your body is not just yours, but also your mate's, and vice-versa. Each of you may have your own complete set of internal organs—a heart, a liver, lungs, kidneys, all your own. However, there is one organ of which you really possess only one half: your genitals. Whether you're an Adam or an Eve, each of you possesses only half of a complete human genital organ, which must include both male and female parts. Therefore, your sexual organ, even if it resides in or on your body, is not just part of your body, but also part of your mate's body. Neither one of your genital organs is complete without the other; indeed, your genitals, more than any other part of your body, are designed for sharing.

For this reason, in a shared-soul marriage, neither one of you has the right to withhold your body from the other, unless there is a serious problem or illness—not one of those fake, manipulative headaches, or "Sorry honey, I'm just not interested." Absolute extreme spiritual sensitivity must be brought into understanding this. Each of you possesses only half of a complete human genital organ, and your spouse needs that half, as you need your spouse's half. Sharing your body with your mate is part of God's order, by virtue of the incompleteness of male and female genitals, by virtue of the shared-soul nature of marriage, and by virtue of the single body of creation with which we are all one. Your body is not just your own; your body is your mate's too.

When you and your spouse understand that your body is not just your own, and that it is God's first, creation's second, yours third, and your mate's fourth, you will no longer fear the other person controlling you or fear losing yourself in the dominant/submissive curse-roles of the past. The right priorities will be in place for you and your spouse to share your bodies the way God intended.

Then you will feel safe to remove your fig leaves and allow any shame or shyness to dissolve between you. You will feel safe opening up—totally opening up—to permit your body to be a gift of God, creation, and yourself, to your mate. In that order!

Your body will become transformed into what it is truly: not just a mass of tissues and teguments, a receptacle or tool for each other's gratification, but a temple for the living presence of God within each of you.

MARRIAGE SECRET #20

The joy of sacred sex

God blessed them, and God said to them,
"Be fruitful and multiply, and fill the earth..."
(Genesis 1:28)

The secrets we have discussed in the previous nineteen chapters have had only one essential purpose: to turn you into a virgin. By "virgin" I do not mean the fleshly meaning of the term, someone who has never had sexual intercourse; to turn you into this kind of virgin may, frankly, be a little too late. By virgin I mean a "spiritual virgin."

A spiritual virgin may have had sexual intercourse, or may not have. A spiritual virgin may be married, intending to marry, not yet married nor ever desiring to marry. Spiritual virgins may be seventeen or ninety-eight years old. Spiritual virgins are human beings who have placed God in charge of their souls, and therefore their bodies. They have reduced, as much as possible, the contamination of a world gone mad, with its politically correct ideas and its fly-by-night sexual values. They have kept serpentine lies from polluting the purity of their spirits and the use of their bodies.

Spiritual virgins are conscious of the fact that the first person with whom they have intercourse is God. From the moment of their birth, if not before, they were "mated" with the Creator. The presence of the Creator penetrated them as their very own soul. Their bodies were aroused first by the Creator's Spirit, who breathed life into them, as into the first human. To spiritual virgins, God is the most beloved, the first and most important lover. And God will always be that, even should they decide to marry and have a fleshly mate.

Spiritual virgins are conscious—deeply conscious—that any relationship they have with anyone, especially their mate, is a relationship between the presence of God within them and that presence within the other. Spiritual virgins are mates of God and, should they offer their body to someone else they love, they do so knowing that their body is the living, tissue-expression of the holiest-of-holy gifts: their souls. They are intimately aware that the body they share with another is God's creation. It is not just their body; it is also God's. When they make love, they are aware, in a very real sense, that it is God making love to God, through the mediating forms of their physical bodies.

For this reason, whether spiritual virgins are Adams or Eves, they know that sexuality is sacred, and approach it that way. Sexuality is not something they, like so many of today's Adams and Eves, parade around with cheap adolescent displays, letting it all hang out with reckless abandon. Spiritual virgins do not allow statistics, peer pressure, media manipulation, or popular culture to determine their sexual behavior. They do not trust these finite, mortal value systems as anything but the serpent's hypnosis.

This, however, does not mean that spiritual virgins are prudes, as they are often cruelly characterized by a sexually obsessed culture. They are not tight, twisted, neurotic creatures, unwilling to share their bodily part of God's creation, even disgusted at the thought. They are simply mature spiritual adults who make their spiritual aspirations more important than sexual desires. With correct spiritual priorities, they have put spirit before body, the Creator before the created, the Formless before the formed. In sexuality, no less than in anything else—perhaps even more so, because it is so very sacred—they have aligned themselves to the order of the Garden.

Now that you are on the road to being spiritual virgins, it's time to consummate your knowledge, to make all the lessons you have learned real and solid, to bring this knowledge into and through your body, to express your soul—your spiritual virginity—for the sacred delight of yourself, your mate, all of creation, and God.

Imagine, right now, that you and your mate are spiritual virgins. You stand before each other naked. Your souls have become aligned to God and the order of creation. You feel no shame. You have worked to create a shared-soul relationship between you as a couple. You are two souls fused as one original human being, although you remain separated into two forms, male and female.

How wondrous! As souls, you've been designed by God to be fitting for each other, like helpmates. As an expression of your souls, your bodies have been designed to be equally fitting, as sexual helpmates. Your "animal skins" can merge together, like pieces of the original Adam. The curves of your bodies were created ergonomically, to follow the curves of your spouse. Your genitals have been designed to interpenetrate and surround each other. Adam's penis enters Eve's vagina as if entering into the depths of the greatest mysteries: the womb of life. Eve's vagina receives its entrance, desiring it, knowing it is potentially the spark of new life. Making love, every Adam is drawn back into the mother from whence he came, every Eve is drawn toward the father who sparked her existence. The cycle of life repeats itself in miniature each time you make love.

When you make love in a spiritual marriage, even if it is a brief moment of sharing, it is not something done to "get it out of the way." It is a sacred offering to God. Like incense in each of your bodily temples, your pleasure ignites between you and rises to God. In holy union between you, your love-making is the most intense of prayers, a "sacrifice" of your life-energy to the God of all existence, a "thank you" sent skyward for the pleasures of this Garden.

Through making love, your minds fuse as one mind. Your bodies fuse into one body, your hearts beating, literally, as one. The cosmic dualities of male and female that permeate all creation and from which the fabric of all phenomena are woven—melt together. The singular image of God, that one image and likeness which includes both male and female, is joined back together. Male and female become indistinguishably one, mirroring the One, shared souls, now fully so, in the flesh.

Through making love, you and your other "half-soul" rejoin. The half-genitals you each possess become whole, each of you completing the other, so that you both share a complete set of human organs. Through you, the original human is restored. The rift between Adam and Eve, the separation and alienation of men and women from each other in our difficult physical life become healed and repaired. Eden, from the root word meaning "pleasure," is literally restored, as your pleasure is released back into Eden through your love-making.

Oneness, that most supreme quality of the Creator, explodes between you as you come together in the act of love-making. Your freedoms as individuals merge into a singular freedom, in devotion to Freedom Itself, the unrestricted, unbounded God. Unbinding your pleasure, your exchange sends waves of goodness through each other and through the entire earth and universe. Oneness, goodness, and freedom, the divine fundamentals upon which the entire order of the Garden is built, become expressed physically, naturally balanced through your super-natural sexual union.

Indeed, through your love-making, all of creation is enlivened. The fluids from your bodies, once the fluids from primeval oceans and rivers, flow gently and, at times, torrentially into each other. The heat from your bodies, which originates from the sun, explodes like solar flares, warming the contours and crevices of your body as the sun does the hills and valleys of earth.

Do you realize that, as one shared soul, as one shared body, you *are* the very act of creation taking place within you? Pause and think about it. A sperm, like a word spoken, is uttered unto the darkness of the deep, and then light—the blazing, illuminating light of life—is released from both of you. Together, as co-creators, you continue the work of Genesis. Through you, the work of creation goes on ... and on. Through you, God creates: as you, through you, by you, along with you, because of you, and for you and everyone.

Yes, it is in the bedroom that everything comes together for a man and a woman and for all creation. Your marriage with each other, your marriage to God, your marriage to all existence join through the act of making love. Sexuality is the most intimate communion between your souls, the sharing of the substance of existence between you.

Sexuality is also the most intimate and authentic communication between you as a couple. It is communication without all the veils or "clothing" of the usual day-to-day intercourse such as talking, arranging, working, and handling the mountain of details life places before us.

How distracted we often become as married couples. How often the problems in life pull us down and tear us away from each other. Living in the same house, we can mindlessly pass each other in the halls and become emotionally disconnected from each other as a couple.

Sometimes there is so much pressure in life from work, from worries, from families and relationships that you feel fractured into many pieces. At times it can get so bad that you may find yourselves in separate corners of the house, unable to talk to each other. At those times, the touch, the caress, the nuzzle, the feel of your enfleshed soul next to your mate's enfleshed soul may be the only words you can speak; they are spoken in a space where even letters and syllables cannot get between you. Making love restores us to the Garden, and to ourselves, bathing us in the love that is the nature of God.

Your so-called "sex life" is far more than a blind, gratuitous exchange of secretions, as so many of today's Adams and Eves see it. It is not a sport in which the goal is frequency or intensity of orgasms. Such artificial standards of performance can make people feel inadequate and anxious about their sexual natures. Sadly, in their liberation from excessive restrictions, today's Adams and Eves have created restrictions in other ways, often reducing sexuality from the heightened spiritual awareness it is to mere lust, a degradation of human spiritual and sexual potential.

Lust is the abandonment of spiritual priorities in sexuality so that self-gratification, self-pleasuring, self-fulfillment, and the satisfaction of your own urges are the only concern. It may feel good; it may feel "hot" and "sexy," as today's Adams and Eves describe it. But, lust—in, of, by, and for itself alone—is, at best, misdirected. When the power of our sex drive is directed in a healthy, loving, spiritual relationship, it is joy, delight, tenderness, and physical

pleasure expressed through mutual sharing and caring. It is
an intensification, a fleshly densification of the spirit the
couple already shares. At its height, such sexual pleasure
can actually become intense passion and even ecstasy—an
almost indistinguishable intermingling of the sensations of
pleasure and pain, the feeling of God's own passion flowing
through your bodies. Such sexual ecstasy will also feel
good, "hot," and "sexy," but it is not lust in the negative
sense of that word, for sexuality is not self-serving, but an
act of physical devotion to what is good and sacred in your
relationship and in God's order.

Our sex drive, no less than any power in creation, must
be *sub-ordinated* (not "squelched under," but "ordered
beneath" or "secondary") to the one power who is the Creator. Otherwise, our sex drive becomes the serpent that
Adam and Eve obey as a separate power from God. This is
why the serpent, a phallus symbol, has often been inter-
preted as representing lust. Sacred sexuality utilizes the
vital power within lust, but it directs this to fuel love, the
love of God expressed as the shared love between you.
Indeed, as many previously promiscuous people have discovered, sacred sex is an even greater joy than the common
lustful variety, precisely because the gift of sexuality is
being used correctly. When aligned to the order of creation, your sexuality is empowered by the entire flow of
God's creation. The force of the Creator aligns to your
own sexual creativity. The entire flow of creation merges
with your sexuality, actualizing it, empowering it, strengthening it, making sacred sex sexier—the ultimate sexual cre-

ativity. Indeed, aligning the power of your sexuality to the power of the Creator will actually improve your sex life. You will have more spirit to share; your love will be intensified. Expressing God's grace through your sexuality will naturally extend foreplay—with no need for Eve to slow or control an overly urgent Adam. Also, the duration of sexual intercourse, and therefore its shared pleasure, will also increase, because the sensual expression of love through touching and tenderness—not merely the release and exchange of fluids—is its spiritual purpose. In short, bringing God into sex improves sex, making it the ultimate physical expression of human creativity.

Remember, you are creative by virtue of being made in the image and likeness of God. As human beings, you are creative in everything you do. There is no reason why your super-natural creative gifts should not be expressed through your sexuality. Indeed, sexuality is the height of creativity— God's own creativity—the very process by which new life is brought into existence. In a deep, consecrated marriage between a man and a woman, creativity—playfulness, curiosity, healthy experimentation—is part of a healthy, human sexual repertoire, part of getting to know each other. It is not sinful; in fact, it is just the opposite. The notion that spiritualized sexuality between a consecrated, monogamous couple needs to be a monotonous and dull, mere "missionary" sex, is a myth. Look below the surface of a dull marriage and you will find people who do not have a spiritual marriage, but merely a "license"; such a marriage is hardly the standard by which to judge marital sexuality.

Nevertheless, in today's excessive environment, which has at times become "overly creative" to the point of violating the order of creation, there are three rules of sexual creativity that must be emphasized and are spiritually non-negotiable. They are self-evident, and yet you'd be amazed at how many of today's Adams and Eves violate them in the name of "sexual freedom":

1. No sexual creativity should hurt, impair, or endanger your physical health or that of your mate. No sexual creativity should violate the integrity of your bodies, which are part of God's creation first and yours second.

2. In sexual creativity, no psychological or physical boundaries should ever be broached without willing, joyful permission and openness on the part of your mate—even if no harm to the person might result. The alternative is rape, whether psychological or physical. It is an intrusion on the other, an intrusion that violates the other person's individuality, unique relationship with God, and spiritual virginity. Women can be raped. But men too can be raped. Rape can happen with a word, or even a thought.

3. Do nothing that violates the sanctity of your conscience. Ever! God's desires come first; your mate's desires come second. Always. Conscience doesn't

mean "inhibition." Conscience means correct use of your body, aligned to your soul. Sexual freedom and conscience, despite what many think, are not polar opposites. They are two aspects of sacred sexuality, inseparably one.

Aside from these three rules, in a spiritually consecrated marriage all the pleasures of Eden are open to you— especially the most remarkable, most wonderful, most intense pleasure of all:

The birth of a child. The living, breathing fact of your union as shared souls and shared bodies. Pleasure-incarnate: a baby.

"Be fruitful and multiply, and fill the earth," God commanded.

May your souls be fruitful; may your spirit multiply in power and vitality; may God's creation go on through you. May you fill the earth with the many joys of sacred sex.

In learning the lessons of the first nineteen marriage secrets, you have worked hard to align your souls to each other. Now, enjoy the alignment of your bodies too.

Consider your orgasm God's gift for all your hard work and attention to your spirit.

V
THE WORLD BEYOND YOU

MARRIAGE SECRET #21

Leave your mother
and father's house

*Therefore a man leaves his father and his mother
and clings to his wife, and they become one flesh.
(Genesis 2:24)*

How many of today's Adams and Eves do you know
who maintain a taut, uncut, steel-reinforced umbilical cord
to their mothers and fathers? There are many signs of this
dangerous spiritual misalignment:

Eves or Adams may be constantly running over to
their parents' house for some little thing, but end
up eating two or three meals a week over there.

Eves or Adams may talk openly to their parents about their spouse and the problems they are having, even before discussing them with their mate.

Eves or Adams may pull energy away from their own family and home with the repeated justification: "My mother (or father) just needs me. What do you want me to do?" (You're then supposed to pity them.)

Eves or Adams may bias their marital or family decisions toward "what's best for my folks" and put themselves last, while patting themselves on the back for being "good children."

Eves or Adams may always be relying on their parents to pick up the slack, especially in the area of finances.

Often, parents play a sizable part in this drama too. Parents who have spent their lives caring for, obsessing over, or controlling their children may find it extremely hard to just let go. They may be terrified of facing an empty nest, unable to deal with the fact that they may be aging. They may fear not having children to distract them, because they may not really want to face each other and deal with the empty marriage they've had all those years, an emptiness that was covered up by having kids. Or, they may simply and innocently not know a proper boundary between themselves and their children because it was not something they learned from their own parents.

When these kinds of parents get a sense, a hint, a whiff, that their married children are disconnecting, living on their own, and no longer clinging to them, they often react inwardly with veiled panic. Seldom will they confront the couple. More often, they will use innuendo to imply that there is a problem and then whine or complain about it. They may handle the disconnection manipulatively by plying the couple with generosity in the form of money, help, and furnishings in order to make their children feel obligated and keep them emotionally connected to themselves. Newlyweds, who tend to be more materially needy, get easily hooked by this technique. It has its desired effect; parental influence, now considerably guilt-laden, intrudes between the young Adam and Eve. This situation begins with newlyweds but often continues for decades in long-standing marriages. The umbilical cord is never severed.

Mothers and fathers who are very skillful at this—and Adams and Eves who are very dependent and don't want to stand on their own two feet—set up a situation in which a couple enjoys being micromanaged *by parents*. Soon, one partner or both can actually forget to cling to their mate and cling to their parents instead. The parents become invisible marital partners.

God makes abundantly clear where your priorities are to lie. No sooner does the Bible describe Adam and Eve as being bone of each other's bone and flesh of each other's flesh than it goes on to draw an apparently odd conclusion: *therefore* they should leave their father and mother's house and cling to each other. In the biblical story, Adam and Eve don't even have a physical body yet. They certainly don't have fathers and mothers; they *are* the first father and mother. This "therefore" feels so out of context in the story that it's hard to imagine why it's actually there. It feels more like a commentary than part of the story line. Indeed, that's exactly what it is: a one-line editorial, designed to deliver one of the Garden's most indispensable lessons. Ignore this one and you condemn to exile not only your marriage, but the entire world.

Because Adams and Eves are each other's bone and flesh, and because future Adams and Eves are also their parents' bone and flesh, having been born from their bodies, the Bible feels an urgent need to establish a decisive, clear boundary line, a divine priority:

> Your mate's flesh goes before your parents' flesh.
> You are more related to your spouse than you are
> to your own parents. Your mate goes before your
> mother or your father. Your household gets prior-
> ity over the household of your parents.

Extending this divine priority beyond parents: your mate goes before your brothers, sisters, aunts, uncles, cousins, and family. Further extending it, your mate goes before your clan, your tribe, your people, your nationality, and indeed, your religion—though your mate might willingly wish to be a part of them. In short, your mate goes before anyone who came before him or her, except God, who came before everyone.

However, in a more general sense, this divine priority has even more profound meaning: since parents precede you, leaving one's parents' house also means leaving the past. It means not letting the past hold you back. It means not being a blind traditionalist but always thinking, innovating, expressing your personal creativity in fresh, exciting, and spiritually uplifting ways. Leaving your parents' house means never letting the past control you, never believing that you must repeat your mistakes, never permitting ties to history to strangle you. It means never, ever, believing that you are condemned to past sins without a "new beginning"—our first marriage secret.

To leave one's parents' house means to live in the now, not in the then. Leaving the past means not allowing your birth to define your destiny. You may have been born poor, but you needn't stay poor. You may have been born of uneducated parents, but you needn't stay uneducated. You may come from an abusive home, but you don't have to be abusive to your mate or be abused by your mate. To leave your parents' house means to seek progress, growth, expansion, movement, forgiveness. It is God saying:

> "Look, I've given you the continual expansion and creative motion of nature and history. Don't stop progress by clinging to what was before. Face forward and create anew."

If a problem should occur, fix it fast and go on. If something is holding you back, let it go and go on. From wherever you are, grow, expand, explore, learn, and reach out to the entire world. To do otherwise is to work against the entire flow of the universe, for you will be putting old before new, prior before next, past before present. You will actually be reversing the flow of time, working against the laws of physics and stifling the infinite possibilities that God is bringing into the world in every next moment.

Such a strange, seemingly misplaced comment in the Bible story. Yet, if we cease leaving our father and mother's house (the past) and cease clinging to our mate (the present), life will cease to expand. This is the secret at the heart of all progress, all advancement, indeed, the entire future of our children and all children. The lesson it contains is of national, world-girdling, even cosmic importance. Think about what would happen if we put this principle into action in all aspects of human civilization:

What would happen if our economic system left our father and mother's house? We might create a new approach to economics that could create greater, more equitable prosperity, not just for our nation, but for the entire world. We might develop an approach to free enterprise that doesn't increase the "haves" at the expense of the "have-nots."

What would happen if we allowed our medical knowledge to leave our father and mother's house? We might develop techniques that aren't worse than the illness for curing diseases such as cancer. We might be more open to spiritual healing as a scientific practice that could save considerable millions in costs.

What would happen if we allowed our social systems to leave our father and mother's house? We could free ourselves from the mistakes of the past, erase the lingering injustices, and liberate whole groups of people into a better future. We might develop more creative unemployment and welfare programs that are more creative than the ones of the past, which enfeebled people, rather than making them self-reliant.

What would happen if we allowed our energy sources to leave our father and mother's house? We might create an infinite supply of energy and never again feel victimized by political winds. We might also be able to preserve and safeguard clean rivers, beautiful forests, and fresh air—God's legacy to all generations.

What would happen if we took every single aspect of human life—from our schools, to the military, to our town centers, to our museums and cultural life, to our inner cities... and freed them all from the restrictions of the past—setting them free from the past, to seek the best, the noblest, the brightest, the most creative, the kindest, the most abundant, the most healing, the most expansive, the most loving, the most life-engendering way of being?

What would happen if we all left our parents' house, and all its mistakes, behind? What would happen if we all clung to our spouse and propagated new possibilities, new thoughts, and a new generation of more positive, more powerful, more uplifting ideas? Can you imagine what we might accomplish?

A monumental task awaits every Adam and Eve if they are brave enough to leave their parents' house and cling to a new vision. This is the task for which you were created. This is the task for which you received the gift of being created in God's image and likeness. The lessons of all the secrets we have discussed have been preparation for this task.

So, steady your nerves. Take a deep breath. Now, with absolute courage, stick just one toe out of your father and mother's house . . . and into the future.

Now you're ready to open your marriage to the world. And the world is ready to open itself to your marriage.

MARRIAGE SECRET #22

Use your gift of dominion

And let them have dominion over the fish of the sea, and over the birds of the air, and over the cattle, and over all . . . the earth.
(Genesis 1:26)

"I do." With these two words, your marriage begins. With these two words you consecrate yourself to each other in the presence of family and friends, in plain sight of community, nation, and, if you've had a spiritual ceremony, God. But "I do" is more than a romantic assent to spend your life together, to "have and to hold, for as long as you both shall live." In a true spiritual marriage, the kind God intended every Adam and Eve to have, "I do" is a solemn pledge—*to do.*

You and your mate, together, were placed here in the Garden *to do*—to create, to accomplish, to till the soil. You

202 ADAM & EVE

were granted what the Bible calls "dominion"—from the Latin, *dominus*, meaning "master" or "lord." You may think that your home is just your tiny piece of the Garden, your fenced-in yard or apartment, but, if you look out of any one of your windows, you'll see how huge your home really is: your home is the entire earth, the sky, the moon, the planets, and the entire universe beyond. The entire world—if not millions of potential worlds—has been entrusted to you and your mate by God. You have dominion. You are the dominant species. You are lords appointed by the Lord, co-creators created by the Creator, masters chosen by the Master. You are granted the super-natural knowledge to shape, mold, bend, and tame this limitless Garden in which we have been placed.

Have you ever stopped to consider the awesome task that God has given you as today's Adams and Eves? The serpent told Adam and Eve that if they ate from the Tree of Knowledge they would be truly lords, masters of the earth. Think about it. You have been granted the power of free will. Every single decision you make—every thought, word, decision, or action—will either increase the freedom, oneness, and goodness built into this world or diminish it. It is as if you are the central column of one of those old-time balance scales, with your arms astride and a plate hanging from each hand. Make a decision that is aligned to God and your dominion blesses the whole world, tipping the scale in the direction of good. Make a decision that is un-aligned to God or, worse, aligned to the serpent, and your dominion curses the whole world, tipping the scale in the direction of evil.

In the past, Adams and Eves and their societies did not fully understand the magnitude of this responsibility. A few millennia ago, human beings were still intellectually quite primitive. They used sticks and stones to subdue the earth; nature seemed a daunting, uncontrollable power. If it snowed, human beings froze. If there was a drought, human beings starved. Humankind felt totally controlled and victimized by the "gods," the forces of nature. People were hardly yet up to the task as lords of creation.

The first thrust of human civilization required humankind to grow more intelligent, more knowledgeable, by taking larger and larger bites of the fruit of the Tree of Knowledge in order to learn how to master nature and be lords over it, not slaves to it. As we can see from the story of Adam and Eve, this began with scratching the ground to raise crops. It was arduous labor and thorns constantly got in the way. But, slowly, Adam and Eve became more savvy. The more they sought to master the natural elements, the more they were rewarded with an astonishing wealth of knowledge about agriculture, biology, astronomy, medicine, physics, mathematics, geology, chemistry, paleontology, archeology—an endless array of disciplines designed to fathom God's design. God's own intelligence and knowledge awoke within us.

As Adams and Eves grew in this knowledge, they rose higher and higher to assume their true spiritual status as lords of nature rather than victims of it. With such increased knowledge, the "curse" of Adam and Eve was increasingly lifted. Labor in the Garden lessened with the invention of mechanical technology; painful childbirth lessened with invention of medical treatment; human beings ceased to resemble ascended apes and began to resemble descended angels. Now, instead of hiding in caves in inclement weather, we were building split-level ranches and skyscrapers. Now we were paving paradise, interconnecting it with roads, importing oranges in the dead of winter, creating irrigation systems to farm deserts, wiring the world, launching satellites, and exploring other galaxies.

Taking still bigger bites of the fruit of the Tree of Knowledge, Adam and Eve ascended in their knowledge of nature so that now that knowledge has truly begun to resemble the knowledge of God, in whose image and likeness we were made. With a "simple" equation, $E = mc^2$, Adam and Eve began to understand how energy could become matter, how spirit could form itself into the material universe. By studying electricity, gravity, and nuclear energy, Adam and Eve slowly peeled away the inner workings of the Creator's mind, learning about the cosmic laws by which God created the world. The forces that in the ancient world had been revered as gods were humbled by Adam and Eve, reduced to mathematics, then piped through copper wires and fiber-optic systems.

Unfortunately, because the first stage of our dominion was an extreme, originating from a desperate need to subdue a seemingly dangerous Garden, we now have the opposite extreme: the Garden is now in danger from us. After a few thousand years, we have decimated nature. We have polluted the air, torn holes in the ozone layer, and induced thermal warming. We have deforested much of the planet, poured carcinogens into the soil, dumped toxic wastes in suburban neighborhoods, and drowned dangerous nuclear wastes into our oceans. Human immunological defenses are breaking down. Sperm counts are plummeting around the world. And, in the ultimate cosmic heresy, which began at Hiroshima, we can now actually take the creational energy that God stored up as matter and release it to destroy creation itself. The atomic bomb essentially reverses creation; it is truly an "anti-God" bomb.

What too many fallen Adams and Eves still do not understand is that dominion does not mean dominance. Dominion does not mean control to the point of being able to exterminate life. Dominion means taking upon oneself the loving, caring task of stewardship for the earth and all of God's creation. Dominion means being lordly by emulating the Lord, being masterful by emulating the Master, acting in the image and likeness of the God who created us. Dominion means permitting the nature of God—God's oneness, freedom, and goodness—to express itself through our doing. Dominion means allowing all the qualities of God to act through us to shape the earth for the benefit of all God's creatures, just as God intended.

Are you up to the task? Are you ready to actually behave as lords? Are you ready to include dominion of the world as part of your marriage vows? Then say, "I do" again—this time, truly understanding the monumental commitment

expressed by these words. These days, more than during any
other period in human history, how you exercise your
dominion will determine the fate of our entire world.

As a spiritual couple, ask yourselves some tough questions about how you are exercising your dominion. Be
nakedly honest in your answers:

> When you purchase a car, do you consider your
> children's lungs as well as the increasing cost to
> society for the medical treatment of respiratory ail-
> ments?

> When you go to the movies, do you feed the finan-
> cial success of gratuitous violence and then feel
> overwhelmed by recent terrorist acts?

> When you buy cleaning fluids, do you stop to think
> about how you will dispose of them and how they
> might affect waterways and wildlife?

> When you build a home, do you consider whether
> it will make others feel loved, welcome, and cared
> for, whether its design will fit harmoniously into
> the environment around it? Or is your main con-
> cern how prestigious it will look?

> If you overeat, do you give any thought to the food
> you could be purchasing and sending to starving
> people instead?

Such questions about dominion penetrate ruthlessly to the soul of your spiritual life as a couple. They are at the core of the large-scale societal issues we are all facing around the world. All of them, without question, are issues of right human dominion:

Education: For what are we educating our children? Are we educating them to make money or to heal the world? Are we educating them for prestige, or to help God's creation? Should the purpose of education be to fill kids with enough facts to pass their SATs or to turn out children of God, who know their task is right dominion?

The Economy: Should every square inch of land and open space be developed? Should ancient, irreplaceable forests be turned into cash crops? Is the economy here to serve just us, or also God and creation? Should the purpose of the free enterprise system be profit or the liberation of people from material restraints so they can spiritually expand? What is right dominion for economists and the economy?

Medicine: Is there a moral limit to medical
                   knowledge? Should we engage in
                   re-engineering our genetics to
                   breed more intelligent humans?
                   Shall we continue to save the phys-
                   ically weak and degrade the genetic
                   vitality of the species? Are doctors
                   God? What is right dominion for
                   physicians and researchers?

Manufacturing: Should children's breakfast cere-
                   als be preserved with carcinogens?
                   Should animals be slaughtered
                   for food without regard to their
                   pain and suffering? What is right
                   dominion for manufacturers and
                   factories?

Agriculture: Do we have the right to geneti-
                   cally alter whole species, grafting
                   insect genes into plants—mixing
                   God's species—just so they will be
                   resistant to cheap weed-killer? Do
                   we have the right to poison cow
                   milk with antibiotics that break
                   down human immune systems?
                   What is right dominion for resear-
                   chers and farmers?

The Arts: Do you think God wants us to
                 release into the consciousness of
                 reality gratuitous violence, mean-
                 ingless sexual indulgence, and
                 anti-social behavior through TV
                 and movies? Are making a profit
                 and satisfying the public's desire
                 in a free society sufficient justifi-
                 cations for the trash on the air-
                 waves? What is right dominion
                 for Hollywood moguls, TV pro-
                 ducers, and writers?

The Media: Should newspapers publish sensa-
                 tionalist, negative tabloids with no
                 journalistic standards? Should our
                 press be motivated simply by high
                 ratings? What is right dominion
                 for journalists and our press?

The Military: Should the stockpiling of atomic
                 weapons be considered "defense"?
                 Do we have the right to geneti-
                 cally alter bacteria in order to cre-
                 ate lethal strains that can wipe out
                 whole populations? What is right
                 dominion for the military and its
                 industrial suppliers?

Politics: Should politicians pander to the
                     population just to get elected, or
                     should their goal be to speak the
                     truth and lead with truth? What is
                     right dominion for elected officials?

Religion: Is it right dominion for religious
                     leaders to pit one group against
                     another, sowing divisiveness rather
                     than oneness throughout society?
                     Do religious beliefs justify vio-
                     lence, ever? If so, when?

There is a lot to right dominion. As a spiritually aligned couple, truly acting like stewards as God commanded you to, you should try to make every decision, whether for your own personal home or the larger home we all share, according to this principle for right dominion:

Dominion—if it is *right* dominion—must enhance oneness, freedom, and goodness for:

You

You and others

The society you share

The world you inhabit, including all that lives

Future generations

In a spiritual marriage, the principle of right dominion must be included in anything you do. Whether the issue is education, window decorating, road construction, food preparation, sexuality, appliance manufacturing, computer design, long-distance telephone service, fashion...ad infinitum...all the urgencies and trivialities of human existence must come under the scrupulous gaze of lords and masters who adhere to the principle of right dominion. Decisions in boardrooms should be governed by this principle; school curricula should be governed by it; government policy should be governed by it; international relations should be governed by it; religions too should be governed by it, although often, sadly, they aren't.

Everything that Adams and Eves do should be done according to this principle of right doing. It is simply a more detailed version of the most fundamental rule of morality there is: *Do unto others, what you would have them do unto you. That which is hateful to you, do not do to another.*

Admittedly, right dominion is not something that is easy. As fleshly creatures, lords or not, all Adams and Eves are weak. We are all hypocrites, author included. My wife and I drive to work in a car that destroys the air. We space out at times in front of the TV without thinking about the sinister garbage we are supporting. Inundated by the values of a fallen world, it is hard to maintain a grip on true dominion, for, indeed, we have actually built up dependencies on that world and its "necessities," and it's often hard to live without them. Sadly, too, we have actually become desensitized to all kinds of "un-right" dominion around us, and unthinkingly often consider them part of normal living.

However, dominion is not something any one couple can accomplish alone. In God's Garden, we are all in it together. As noted earlier, all of us are totally dependent. The responsibility for lordly, masterful stewardship of this earth does not fall just to you, but includes you and everyone else. True stewardship requires that you join with other couples and organize so that the full burden of dominion is shared—as it should be—among all pieces of the original human. Shared dominion is a shared human task, part of the "marriage" that includes all humanity, our marriage to God and creation.

Even if it may be difficult to exercise our dominion perfectly—exactly as God would—we can certainly do our best. In any given circumstance, including all the practical matters, all we need to do is our best, and then raise the benchmark and do better the next time. All we need to do is better still, and then raise the benchmark and do even better after that. If every Adam and Eve would continuously apply the principle of right dominion to everything they do, and keep improving and improving, then, over time, true lordly dominion by human beings would reshape the world.

God wanted human beings to "subdue the earth." However, in today's world, we must also subdue ourselves. Although we are lords and masters, we are not *the* Lord and Master, but merely a fleshly creation, fashioned in God's image and likeness. We have tremendous power and knowledge, but we still desperately need God's wisdom and guidance to exercise these gifts properly.

So, enjoy your lordly power. Use your gift of dominion. Let every one of today's Adams and Eves say "I do" with gusto, and then *do*. But, as a spiritual couple, seeking to align yourselves with God and creation, exercise your dominion at home or out in the world with two "c's": *caution* and *care*. And don't ever forget:

> It is God's world first, and ours only second. What we do with it depends upon the most powerful "c" of all: our *choice*.

Choose wisely.

MARRIAGE SECRET #23

Solve problems with creativity

And whatever the man called every living creature,
that was its name.
(Genesis 2:19)

As we discovered in discussing Marriage Secret #5, *the* hallmark of Adam and Eve's super-natural inheritance, the *sine qua non* of being made in the image and likeness of God, is creativity.

There is no creature in God's Garden that is as creative as human beings. Human creativity can be seen in everything we do and are. There are more human creative expressions of language, art, literature, science, mathematics, and social science than the largest library could ever hold. Indeed, creativity is built into the very physical nature of Adam and Eve. There are Adams and Eves who are brown, pink, yellowish, and reddish; there are Adams and Eves who are dwarfs or Watusis, narrow-nosed, wide-nosed, blonde, brunette, or redhead; there is more creative diversity in the human species than in any other creature in the Garden. Even below the skin, human creativity is pronounced. For instance, there are more independently moving facial muscles in the human than in any other animal. These muscles are capable of creating an astonishing array of creative expressions: laughing, scowling, crying, and rage. In the human brain, there are more creative interconnections between nerve cells than there are in any other animal, which is why our brain is capable of advanced creative thought and extraordinary flights of fantasy. We are also capable of vaulting the heavens and bringing back such spiritual ideas as beauty, truth, and harmony. We can use these divine ideas as guiding principles for creatively designing our civilization.

Creative thinking is the ability to think symbolically. Adam and Eve, unlike any other creature in the Garden, can see something, such as a tree, and connect it with a deeper meaning—its sturdy trunk representing the concept of strength, its shade-bearing foliage representing the concept of protection. Such conceptual thinking was part of the soul-nature of the original Adam, as shown when God paraded the animals in front of Adam and had him name them. To name an animal, Adam had to be able to: see the animal; differentiate it from other animals; sense, feel, or intuit the nature of the animal; and creatively harness language symbols to create a name for the animal. Adam and Eve's ability to use symbolic language meant they had power—power over the earth, power over other life, dominion.

Creativity *is* power! Creativity is the power to shape human civilization, the power to shape the earth, the power to utilize things, plants, or animals to serve human needs or visions. Creativity is the power to shape one's life. Creativity is pure conceptual power—the power to release ideas and give them physical form. Like God, we conceive of a thought, express it as an idea or word, release it into reality, and then, with a flurry of spirit, organize a myriad of activities around that word, until—lo and behold—what was once an idea, conceived in the womb of our minds, becomes an actual thing. The same creative process that God displayed in Genesis resides within us, although not on the same scale.

Even things that, according to the surface laws of nature, initially appear to be impossible are rendered not only possible, but actual, because of the divine power of human creativity:

Throw a lump of steel in water and it sinks.

However, use your creative mind to fathom a higher law of nature, and that same lump of steel can be turned into a super-tanker or a jet, floating in the sea or the air.

All human invention—everything from a nuclear reactor to a candy bar—is created by human beings understanding the laws of God's creation and using those laws to serve their needs. We take creativity for granted, but it should never be taken for granted. It is, in fact, holy. When you create, you actually draw down a portion of God's own intelligence and direct it. The unknown becomes known to you. God's own knowledge of nature is revealed to you as your own growing human knowledge. When you are creative, you are actually expanding spiritually; you are, in a sense, gods who are becoming more God.

Because creativity requires you to seek knowledge from beyond, it is, in a very real sense, a form of prayer, which we'll discuss in the next chapter. When you are creating, you are seeking beyond yourself to find an inspiration or revelation, often to solve a problem. You are stretching your mind to encompass more of God's mind and, in that sense, seeking God's help. From such creative prayers was created the polio vaccine that saved millions of lives. From such creative prayers was created the heart-lung machine that surgeons could use to repair torn cardiac muscle. Every search to fulfill human needs as well as the inspired inventions that came as a result were forms of creative prayer being answered by a higher intelligence.

Creativity is the naturally human, super-naturally divine way to solve problems:

Think about any problem you may be having right now.

Think about how you are banging your head over it.

Think how you are struggling to solve the problem, but just can't do it.

Think about how your frustration and worry are
growing the longer the problem persists and the
more its solution evades you.

Creativity is the answer.

Problems often arise because people allow their serpent-
mind with its reptilian brain to take over. The serpent-
mind tricks us into seeing our world split into "this" and
"that," "good" and "bad," "positive" and "negative." "either
or." Our primitive rational brains carve up creation into
opposing forces. Instead of seeing the world through the
singular lens of God's love and oneness, we see divisiveness,
discord, and duality instead. Acting upon this view of reality, we actually sow and reap this view in the flesh, creating
real-life problems that originated in our mind and its fractured perceptions.

Our serpent-mind has created all the mental fracture-
lines that sowed the problems we currently experience in our
world. Our serpent-mind has made "haves" opposite to
"have nots," males opposite to females, whites opposite to
blacks, poverty opposite to wealth, children opposite to
adults, law and order opposite to chaos, democracy opposite
to authority, economic well-being opposite to environmen-
talism, military security opposite to disarmament, ghettos
opposite to suburbs. We create many huge problems because
our minds are polarized, so we see two diametrically opposed

views in conflict and turn our world into a contest between "good guys" and "bad guys," with all of us sandwiched in the middle. As a couple, any time your minds are polarized, you contribute to the divided state of the world. How fractured is the way you see the world right now?

Problems also arise because, as spiritual beings, we are constantly growing and changing. What worked in the past, and worked well, may not necessarily work now or in the future. Since we are all part of a creative universe, with newness taking place every nanosecond of our existence, we are continuously challenged to go beyond our old ways of doing things. Indeed, when problems arise, it is often because we have failed to recognize that we've gotten trapped in our old ideas and have failed to be creative, failed to permit changes that needed to take place; we have stayed in our parents' house.

We may resist creativity out of fear or laziness. We may resist creativity because we are concerned that something new may disturb the people around us who've grown dependent on our old way of doing things. This kind of resistance causes exile from Eden, because we are essentially valuing old habits more than new beginnings, and the order of creation does not tolerate that. We have actually deified our old ways of doing things, turned them into little gods that we do not question. Such false gods—our own finite beliefs—when worshiped, lead us astray, right down the road to serious problems in our lives. These problems are a sign from God that we must dispense with our old gods and move on. In fact, virtually all problems are a sign

that we have, in some fashion, disconnected from God—
and a disconnection from God means a disconnection from
creativity itself.

Do you want to solve some of the problems in your
life? Do you want to help solve some of the problems in the
world? Then follow these easy steps, and start thinking creatively—like the Creator in whose image and likeness
you're made:

> 1. Take a look at any problem you have and, rather
> than seeing it as a problem, see it as a creative chal-
> lenge from God to create something new and bet-
> ter. Problems cease to be problems the moment
> you view them as challenges. This is how you acti-
> vate God's grace to handle any difficulties that con-
> front you.

> 2. Try not to look at the problem as something
> happening to you, something outside you. Instead,
> utilizing Adam and Eve's conceptual power, try to
> look at the problem symbolically. What does the
> problem, as a symbol, represent to you? What is
> the message this problem is trying to tell you about
> yourself? What is the meaning of the problem?
> What is God trying to tell you about where you're
> stuck—and where you need to go?

> 3. After you and your helpmate have identified the
> blessing within your curse (and every curse *is* a

blessing in disguise), allow yourselves to play. Like innocent babes in the Garden, let your imagination fly. Let go of the box you've locked yourself into. Imagine and envision a creative solution to the problem. Make it fun, because that opens the door to fresh ways of thinking—childlike, pure, and "un-adult-erated," without rigid "have to's."

4. Then, whatever the solution that dawns on you, don't hesitate. Put it into action. Do something—anything—to set the new creative idea in motion, making it instantly real. This will plant the seed of the solution firmly in the Garden of God's mind.

5. Finally, water the seed of the solution with more creative thought and more deliberate actions. Look for signs that God is helping you solve your problem. If you stay awake, you will notice all sorts of people and conditions coming to your aid to help your solution get rooted. The moment you plant a creative prayer, it begins to sprout. It is only a matter of time before your problem disappears, because the seed you planted in God's mind will become a living, thriving plant, bearing fruit. This is grace in action.

These five steps are a very simple technique for a creative prayer through which you dream up the solution, sow it in God's Garden, and allow God to help you reap the

results. It is human imagination in action, creative dominion and the exercise of your super-natural power as conceptual beings.

However, sometimes Adams and Eves can be so stuck
with a problem, so locked in a box, that they can't envision
a way out of it. When I counsel married couples who seem
glued to problems, I challenge them with an imaginative
exercise, which, at first, seems crazy to them. In fact, they
often look rather startled when they hear it:

> "OK. Right now I have placed a magic wand in
> your hand. You can solve your problem instantly,
> without worrying about how your solution will
> affect people you love, and without worrying about
> whether you will be creating any new problems.
> Go ahead. Wave the magic wand. What do you
> want?"

It is absolutely remarkable. More often than not, to
what seemed like an insurmountable problem the couple
already had an answer, but they were afraid to take a leap of
faith and trust their instincts. In their hearts they already
had a creative answer to their dilemma, but they were simply afraid to "let go and let God," permitting a new wave of
creativity to wash the problem from their lives. However,
the moment I gave them an imaginary exercise, they
"switched brains," turning away from the divisive serpent-
mind, and turning toward their God-blessed creative mind.
Then the solution surfaced, like magic. Their problem

became un-knotted through the power of their creativity. The wand worked, because the "magic," God's own creativity, was already inside them as co-creators.

Sometimes creative solutions come consciously, as a sudden "Aha," a "Eureka." But at other times they take longer, and you can't force them. You have to allow the solution to stew in your subconscious mind, gestating, like a baby, until the inspiration is ready to be born. When I want to help my subconscious mind solve a problem, what I do is imagine the problem going up to the sky, like a white dove, or a balloon, sailing up to God. Then I just forget about the problem. I leave it alone and don't obsess over it. What happens, generally quite quickly (because I've practiced), is that an answer to the problem seems to be created behind the scenes, dawning at the strangest times, when I least expect it. Sometimes I myself don't come up with the solution; it is provided by others. Then it feels as though a mind greater than mine has been solving the problem for me, coordinating with others to help me.

Because creativity is the use of a higher mind within you, drawing upon inspiration from a source beyond the merely human, the solution you get to a problem may surprise you. The inspired idea may make no sense in terms of rational understanding; in fact, it may seem like nonsense. However, something happens—mysteriously—when you use your divine creativity. You get a feeling, a kind of inner click, when the creative solution to a problem dawns on you. It's a knowing that surpasses your usual knowing—an inspired gut-feeling that envelops all of you: mind, feelings, will, and body. You sense an impulse, a sudden urge to act. Your intuition knows it's right. This is the feeling of creativity combined with grace. All the different sides of you, all the different polarities and conflicts inside you are harmonized into oneness, pushed out into a single thrust— from you into the world.

Release that impulse, release your creative power, trust it, and you will see your problem clearing away right before your eyes. Never accept a problem as a defeat—as the limitation of the serpent. Offer it up to the light of creativity in you and the obstacles will dissolve through a motion of creative spirit.

In the timeless words of one of the most spiritually inspired blockbusters of all times: "May the Force be with you." The Force of the Creator. The creative force within you.

MARRIAGE SECRET #24

Make decisions through prayer

The LORD God took the man and put him in the Garden of Eden
to till it and keep it.
(Genesis 2:15)

In the last chapter, we spoke about creative prayer, the kind of prayer that helps when you have an idea, a concept, or a vision you wish to make real on earth. It can be a business, a charitable idea, a scientific invention—any human desire—that you wish to sow and reap. In creative prayer, you start off with some preconceived purpose in mind, some personal goal you wish to accomplish, some problem you wish to solve. Any creative goal is a prayer, because nothing you ever accomplish is accomplished by you alone. It requires the mechanics of all creation, the interaction of an inconceivable number of people and events, for any single act of human creativity to come to fruition. The coordination of all these factors, in total dependency, is impossible without God. This is why creativity is truly a form of prayer, though most people don't think of it that way. In fact, if you speak to people who have accomplished extraordinary things, you'll often hear about the strange coincidences and "good fortune" that helped them achieve it. Simply put, their creative prayer was answered—by God.

However, if all there was to prayer was reaping the creative consequences of our own planting, then this would, in effect, be a godless universe. We might think that *we* are God—totally, and absolutely—and that God is just some impersonal force, some mere substance or quantum field whose sole purpose is to be shaped by our desires, for our desires alone.

Certainly, prayer, in the form of creatively sowing and reaping our desires, is part of the biblical viewpoint. However, prayer is a much deeper phenomenon than mere wish fulfillment. It goes way beyond telling God what we'd like to do or get. It goes way beyond some whisper in the ear of some "Santa-god." Prayer—deep, soulful prayer—penetrates into the mysterious heart of God. It is a mystery, a sharing, a communion with God in mind, body, soul, spirit, and total existence. Prayer is the supreme act of knowing between God and you. Like sacred sexuality between Adam and Eve, it could be said to be intercourse between you and God: you join bodily and spiritually with God, make your sacred boundaries permeable, and allow yourselves to bask in God's presence.

More than asking God for what you want, prayer is asking God for what God wants. Prayer is . . .

> God seeking you.
>
> God making you.
>
> God informing you.
>
> God instructing you.
>
> God leading you.
>
> God guiding you. And, most important,
>
> God loving you.

In true prayer, you do not have any preconceived agenda. You are not creating; God is. It is not your idea you are seeking; it is God's idea. You are not petitioning God; God is petitioning you. You are not desiring your intention, but desiring only God's intention. You are not expressing your need, your will, your thought, your creative desire. You are seeking God's will, God's thought, God's creative desire. You have opened yourself up, putting aside, as best you can, your personal agendas. You are actively seeking to make yourself into an instrument, a servant, a consecrated human, a devoted child, a vessel through which God's will is done. You are no longer the sower and reaper. You, and your marriage, become the ground for God's sowing and reaping, the fertile soil for God's creativity, for what God wishes to accomplish through you.

Prayer in this sense is surrendering, from the Old French *sur-rendre*, meaning to "give up." It is not a forfeit, defeat, or loss of your conscious self, but a rendering upwards, skywards, a giving over and beyond to God to direct your way. Prayerful surrender is the easiest way to make any decision in your life. Through prayerful surrender, decisions become easier because, rather than using your serpentine mind to manipulate this or that, trying to coordinate this or that person, trying to weigh and foresee all the events that may issue forth from any decision—you simply go to the Master Mind to manage them all. Prayerful surrender is "one-stop-shopping," so to speak. You prayerfully surrender to God. Then, trusting God completely, with an innocent, open heart, you permit God to move all the pieces the way God needs them to move. You do not so much *make* the correct decision as permit yourself to *be led* to the correct decision. And, because God is doing the leading, it is the correct decision for all creation—which also, fortunately, includes you. Prayerful surrender makes life easier, because it's the simple, conscious return to the unfallen state of the original couple, your human decision to reverse their curse and obey God's order.

In prayerful surrender, God reads the innermost thoughts of your heart and directs your decision for the betterment of all. Communing deep within the silence of your being, you may hear a voice. You may hear an actual verbal suggestion or resounding command. Or, perhaps, some image will come to mind that has a certain meaning to you, implying a certain message. You may also hear or see nothing, but feel something within you—a greater sense of harmony and oneness, as if the confusion in your decision-making process has given way to a certain peace. Perhaps you will not feel anything at all, and the whole experience will feel like a waste, when, in fact, the surrender is working deep within you, below the level of your conscious or even subconscious mind, and so you are unaware of its effect. Regardless, it's important to never enter prayerful surrender with any expectations whatsoever, because that's controlling God, which is hardly surrender. Surrender means simply accepting what happens, naturally and effortlessly.

There's only one critical caution if you and your spouse wish to make decisions through prayerful surrender: *Be careful to whom you surrender.* When you are relinquishing yourself to a power beyond you, you cannot always be sure that this power is *the* Power. There are many complex psychological factors that interface in prayerful surrender. Many a mad-Adam and mad-Eve have heard a voice commanding them to commit great atrocities or self-mutilation and assumed that the voice was God's. So, always stay clear, rational, and dust-humble. Should you hear any guidance, always ask yourself: Is this going to harm anyone—including myself—in any way? Is this loving? The answers to these questions will help you determine whether you are spiritually advanced enough for prayerful surrender, or they may indicate that you need to seek advice from spiritually aware clergy or counselors.

Spiritually advanced or not, many Adams and Eves may never feel comfortable making their decisions through prayerful surrender, even if they try practicing it for some time. It may make them feel a little disconnected from basic human life, more monkish than married. It may feel unnaturally passive. They may wish to reserve such deep surrender for moments of meditation and reflection, or for core life decisions or traumatic events. That's OK. Your relationship to God is not a contest, and no one wins kudos for degrees of surrender. God answers your prayer perfectly at your own level. Every prayer you make is answered in accordance with your nature, your beliefs, your education, your necessities, and your lifestyle. In short, it's OK to be you and to pray your way. God doesn't require you to be someone else. Otherwise, you'd have been born with someone else's soul.

If prayerful surrender does feel a bit extreme for you, you may prefer a simple practical method for permitting God to direct your path, with the same kind of assurance, but in a way that relates more to your way of life. May I suggest then, a technique that I just "accidentally" (nothing is an accident, in God's universe) discovered, when my wife and I were having difficulties making decisions. I call it the Rule of Four. It starts like this:

> If you and your mate have a decision to make, either individually, or together, *never, ever* make it unless three people agree: you, your spouse, and you and your spouse together.

No matter what the decision (except in an imminent life-threatening situation, where there's no time to wait), you are not to make the decision unless the three of you are in complete, absolute agreement—*always*. In the event that you can't come to an agreement, even after working hard to convince the other of your point of view, even after gathering as much information as possible to persuade yourself and the other—then, proceed to the Rule of Four:

> Refusing to make the decision, now include *four people* in the agreement: you, your spouse, you and your spouse together, and God.

> The Rule of Four means you simply admit: "Well, I guess God doesn't want us to make the decision yet. There's probably something we're both missing. After all, we've got only a finite bit of knowledge, and we can't seem to reflect Oneness yet in our decision. So, let's agree to make only one decision for now: *Let's wait and see what God has in mind.*"

It is really amazing. If, instead of fighting over making a decision, you simply don't force it, but rather open up and allow God to lead you, you will notice something miraculous. Over the course of the next few hours, or days, or however long it takes, God will send you people, advice, information, and all sorts of new inspirations to help you make your decision—unanimously. You will notice that everything you need to effortlessly arrive at a mutual decision, in perfect timing for the mutual benefit of you and your mate, will be sent. Try it. It works. It's easy.

Moreover—and this is absolutely thrilling—with the Rule of Four, you and your mate can actually dispense with the usual marital "wisdom": You can have a marriage *without compromise*. In fallen-marriage advice, which doesn't take into account spiritual principles, compromise is actually considered the foundation of a good marriage. One person gives up so the other can get, or vice-versa. To my mind, all this does is create two portions of 50 percent happiness, rather than a double-portion of 100 percent. If you practice the Rule of Four, you'll discover that you don't have to compromise, ever, in marriage. As long as you are willing to wait for God to settle any differences between you, a way will open up for you both to have your way, without either one losing or winning: a spiritual win-win for you both. Indeed, you may discover that you never have an argument again.

The Rule of Four works not just for your personal decisions but also for decisions in business, community relations, charitable work, or any of your dominion-related activities. It can actually create unanimous decisions between any number of people, avoiding the problem with majority rule, which, no matter how democratic, often just averages guesses (however educated) and doesn't permit God to rule.

However, the Rule of Four does require one thing from its practitioners: patience. You must wait on the Lord. In today's hyper-speed Garden, where everything seems to be done in terms of hard deadlines rather than easier "living-lines," patience is not easy to come by. But, as you implement the Rule of Four, patience actually develops. You begin to notice that you're making the right decisions more often, and that you're no longer wasting a lot of time in blind alleys or dead ends or having to correct problems caused by rushed, shortsighted decisions. Although the Rule of Four requires a little more time and patience up-front, you more than make up for it in efficiency, ease, and lack of blunders on the back end.

Life in the Garden is full of decisions. No one can go a single day without making one and, in fact, we're making decisions with every flutter of thought that whisks through us.

But, no matter what decisions cross your plate, you don't have to make them alone. You don't have to scratch your heads or wring your hands. Always remember, you have a God—a real, personal God—upon whom you can call to help you make every decision correctly.

Pray. Get answered. Decide. There is nothing easier than to trust God.

MARRIAGE SECRET #25

Your work is sacred

By the sweat of your face you shall eat bread
until you return to the ground.
(Genesis 3:19)

Every day, millions of Adams and Eves return home from their jobs. If you were to eavesdrop on their comments, or listen more carefully to your own, you might hear the following:

"I can't stand that place. It's driving me crazy."

"You won't believe what that jerk did to me."

"Why did I ever do this with my life?"

"Two more years, honey—tops—and I'm outta there."

Their jobs, into which they put virtually all of their daily energy, more than half their soul's life-span, have become a prison, a living hell. How do such nightmares happen?

Everyone's story is always a little different. But, generally speaking, Adams and Eves fall into this curse because they believe they have to. Instead of living according to spiritual priorities, they become lured by the serpent and buy into a false value system. I should know. It happened to me once and, from time to time, the serpent still tricks me with his more notorious lies:

Power over others is the key to control over my life.

Prestige will make me feel successful and safe.

I'll put in forty-five years, and then at sixty-five I'll be free.

I've got to sacrifice for the family at the expense of my own happiness.

And the lie that generally undergirds all such lies:

Money is freedom. The more I have the more free I'll be.

Because of the false values of this world, most of us are tricked into thinking of money as the very purpose of our job. We are often willing to sell our job-joy for a buck, and therefore we purchase our own misery. Trusting the almighty dollar over the Almighty, we make money an idol, believing that it—instead of God—is the source of our happiness and support. We learn to believe that we must actually sell our spirit for the sake of practicality, thereby, once again, reversing the order of Genesis, putting the material before the spiritual, creation before the Creator, and repeating the mistake of the biblical couple. We don't really believe that if we have the faith to seek job-joy, God will guide us toward finding it. Eventually, such misplaced faith, like the serpent in the story, is condemned to grovel in the dust. If, for some reason, our supply of money is cut off due to a firing, an unexpected economic downturn, or some competitor beating us at the "game," we often end up feeling hopeless, helpless, and empty. We question the meaning of it all. We reap the curse of an idolater's life, stuck in a rut, rather than the blessing of being a free child of God's grace. This happens to individuals and couples. This happens throughout society.

God did not intend your life to be one of futile labor, scratching the ground to bring forth thorns, a miserable, self-enslaving job that makes you feel cursed and banished from the goodness of the Garden. For those Adams and Eves who wish to shed the serpent's hypnosis, such a curse can be easily reversed:

> Choose the job you like to do, and stop worrying about money. Let God "worry" about the money for you.

When you choose the kind of job that will bring you happiness, you put money in its right and proper place. Money no longer becomes the purpose of your job, but simply an enjoyable by-product of it. No longer is money an idol to which you're enslaved. Instead, money is recognized for what it really is: a petty "god" of human invention that you—through your conscious choice to seek what is more important—have made subordinate to the only God. Choosing the freedom of God, not enslavement to mammon—you have defiantly declared your human freedom. You have decided to express your daily activity in happiness, not misery. You have let go of the desperate fear of the exiled couple who felt banished from God's support, turned into beasts of labor. You have reasserted your nobility as God's super-natural creation. You have turned to God, and declared:

> "We refuse to believe that we must live lives in silent desperation like a cast-out couple. We trust you to direct us to a better job, and take care of the money too."

When you trust God's freedom, miracles begin to happen in your life. God answers your faith. Such faith suddenly throws open a thousand doors, possibilities that you had not dreamt were possible. Strange, unusual coincidences begin to take place, coincidences that will miraculously guide you away from the job you hate toward a much better job. Indeed, you will notice that soon, not only will you have a job you love—or, at least, one you love more—but the concern over money that was keeping you from changing will also dissolve. God sends you the money, like a cherry on a sundae—an "added perk"—a reward for living up to the dignity of being created in the divine image and likeness and approaching life with faith, not fear.

Many Adams and Eves who have been stuck in unhappy, miserable jobs, thinking there is no way out, have tested the waters of freedom. They have discovered that life is safe. They have discovered that God provides for them monetarily, no less than God provided for the biblical couple by supplying "every plant yielding seed" and "every tree with seed in its fruit"—as long as they stayed aligned to the order of the Garden. Although the agriculture in our Garden is no longer primitive like that practiced in the Garden of the biblical couple, it is still a "human-made agriculture," one of sowing and reaping products and ideas in our economy, and the spiritual law governing supply and abundance is the same: trust God and the spirit that's implanted in you, and you will be provided for. Seek the serpent, and you will end up laboring in the fields. Sell your freedom, thereby violating your spiritual nature, and you will have less to show for it. Relish your freedom and express it with abandon, and you will have more. Upon these spiritual laws our entire free-enterprise system is founded. It works because a free system is usually for the most part aligned to the natural law of the Garden.

If you're like most spiritual couples, the more you discover that money never stands in the way of getting a job you love, the more you will find that a deeper, more spiritual challenge begins to emerge in your shared life. As you notice that your bills are paid, and the needs of your children are being taken care of, and, as the expression goes, "God provides," what will concern you is not just a job but something of truly greater significance—one of the most profound and powerful spiritual ideas: *work*—in the deep, spiritual meaning of that word.

Work is not just a "job," even if you happen to like it. Work, in a spiritual sense, goes way beyond supporting yourself or enjoying your day. Work is one of the most sacred human activities and, ideally, every job should be work, and it is work that should be your job.

When Adam and Eve fell into physical life, God required work. No longer could they rely, like innocent children, upon their Divine Parent to take care of them without their active participation. Something had changed. They had bitten off a piece of God's own knowledge. They were suddenly thrust into conscious awareness of good and evil and, therefore, of their awesome responsibilities as co-creators of the Garden.

Work was a natural outcome of this new knowledge. A portion of God's knowledge was now concentrated within them. It could not remain dormant, for that would be like holding back the power of God within them. Indeed, it was absolutely imperative for the biblical couple to get to work. Only by working could Adam and Eve truly understand their super-natural capabilities. Only by working with free will could Adam and Eve discover how to use their newly found power in a way that was aligned to God's order.

Work, in this sense, is the foundation of all human dominion, and dominion could not exist without it. It is more than mere labor, or a job; it is a spiritual offering to God. Work is the material expression of God's Spirit, which, having been implanted within you, is released back to creation for the sake of goodness. For this reason, the Hebrew word for "work," *avodah*, means both "work" and "service," as in a temple sacrifice. Work is truly a *sacrifice*, a "sacred making," as the word literally means, a devotion of your life's energy to God's order. Whereas a job is often merely a service to yourself, or your company, work is always service to God. It is a deeper, richer, more expansive act, touching on all levels of God's creation.

Work is, in principle, your personal contribution to God's creation, your offering to the entire universe. At its highest, through work, you completely open up your soul to the Lord of creation—surrendering unconditionally, permitting God to work through you as an instrument to accomplish the continuing act of creation through your hands. Thus, hardly a curse, work is a cosmic blessing, the power of human beings merged with the power of the Creator to accomplish a shared purpose: a good, kind, and noble human life in harmony with God's world, at peace with all humanity, all creatures on the earth, and the earth itself.

No wonder work is considered, by all the world's greatest religions, to be redemptive. It is through work that human beings actually become human. It is through work that human beings rise to express their super-natural natures and fulfill their sacred tasks. It is through work that we redeem ourselves from being ascended apes and raise ourselves to knowing what we really are: descended angels.

Think about your current employment. What do you currently do for a living? Is it work, in a spiritual sense? There is little doubt that you already are at work, in a spiritual sense, even if you don't realize it. For instance, let's say you work on an assembly line, manufacturing nails. Can you just imagine the families that would go homeless without your work? Can you just imagine what the lives of children would be like without your nails to hold a roof over their heads? Oftentimes, the difference between "a job" and "spiritual work" is realizing—truly realizing—the enormous impact that your job-work has on the lives of everyone in creation.

Sadly, most Adams and Eves fail to stop and honor themselves for their hard work and commitment, even if their jobs aren't always a pleasure. Employees in a plant that manufactures nails may have taken the job because they needed income, or because the factory was in their neighborhood. But what would happen if, raising their spiritual consciousness, they were to have taken the job knowing in advance that it was truly an offering to God, their contribution to providing homes for people all over the world? What would happen? They would go to work with an entirely different attitude. Even though they might have blue-collar jobs—which this twisted, fallen society considers second rate and low class

—they would arrive at work with a true sense of spiritual importance. Their labor would not be merely a mechanical instrument to make stockholders and CEOs wealthy, something without real meaning, easily replaceable by a machine when economically advantageous. They would view their labor as a divine instrument for helping the world.

If everyone in the world approached their work *as work*, in a spiritual sense, the entire economy would shift. The quality of our labor would increase, the accomplishments of industry would improve, the GNP would rise—all because we would treat everything our hands touch as an offering to God. The respect we accord ourselves would be so high that we might not need to organize into coercive unions to pressure management into respecting us. We would radiate self-respect, on the order of God, not institutions. We would cease to treat ourselves as common laborers, degrading our labor as something beneath us, or beneath others. We would cease to judge our achievements by the fallen standards of the world, but see them in terms of more secure spiritual standards.

Indeed, it is from understanding the meaning of work as a spiritual idea that we gain a truly spiritual work ethic. When companies or nations try to impress upon workers the need to have a "good work ethic" to augment productivity, they are not speaking of a work ethic in the spiritual sense. The kind of work ethic to which they are referring peters out over time, because a true work ethic cannot be pushed or coerced. You cannot hammer it into the psyches of workers, conditioning them like dogs. With a true work ethic, you are not working because some boss is standing over your shoulder and watching your contribution to the bottom line. You are not motivated by fear or by mere responsibility to the group, or even by your self-interested desire to advance or climb the career ladder. With a true work ethic you do a good job because you know it is also God's job. You realize that your work is a spiritual devotion to God. Your pride results from your knowing that you are a physical image of the God who made you. Such a work ethic, based on the burning passion of a truly spiritualized worker, can never be extinguished. It spreads from person to couple, to society, to the entire world.

What would our economy be like if it were organized according to a true work ethic? What would our world be like? When work is understood for what it really is, a spiritual devotion to God, the potential exists to totally reshape our lives personally and collectively:

> With a true work ethic, the way you deal with co-workers is part of your sacred responsibility to God. Ruthless competition is a betrayal of the Creator—for it means taking delight in your success at the expense of another. On the other hand, cooperation between co-workers, between companies, between nations, is a blessing. Such economics does not divide people, but unites people, increasing oneness in the Garden.

With a true work ethic, you do not only consider the ends you wish to attain, but also the means. Purpose—God's purpose—is always put before profits. Corporate policy and spiritual truth are inseparable. "Just winning" regardless of the spiritual cost is the serpent's lie.

With a true work ethic, a top spiritual priority is honoring your employees, not pressuring them unhealthily for deadlines or bottom lines. After all, you should never mistreat any of God's children by enslaving them for your profit. Besides, if they have a true work ethic, you won't have to pressure them or yourself. They'll do their best—for God, not you.

With a true work ethic, the work of your hands, or of your company, must never betray society or the Garden we all share. The principle of right dominion must become etched in the consciousness of all workers, whatever their particular jobs.

Work is truly the greatest human challenge—God's challenge to us after we nibbled on the fruit of the Tree of Knowledge. It is through our work that we contribute ugliness or beauty, success or failure to ourselves and others. It is through work that we either help or hinder those around us. It is through work that we either aid God's goodness or inhibit God's goodness, accelerating our return to or banishment from Eden.

In short, work is how God teaches us to care, and care is the reason we work. Indeed, care *is* work, and work *is* care. Working is caring for ourselves, our mates, our families, our neighbors, our society, and our world. Working is caring—and caring deeply—in a way that could never be adequately measured by a paycheck or by stock performance. It was because Adam and Eve hadn't learned to care about God's order that they broke it. By requiring Adam and Eve to work, to interact with nature in order to contribute to their keep—God forced them to learn to care. By forcing us to care, God forces us to spiritually grow up. Is there any child who can fully understand her parents before she gets out into the world and starts working for a living? By working/caring, every child of God learns to appreciate his Divine Parent. By working/caring, every child of God begins to gain an adult appreciation for the incredible Work of creation that God has handed us—to be handled, by us, with care.

At its simplest, but most profound: *work is how adults love God.* Through work, we go beyond an innocent child-like love of God and express an adult love of God: fiery, powerful, purposeful, dedicated, devoted, and focused on action, healing, and good works. Through work, we turn our love of God into adult actions that demonstrate our love and care for ourselves, others, creation, and the divinity housed within everything. Without work, love for God is a mere romance, a fiction, a nebulous feeling that makes for pretty poetry or childhood lullabies, but that accomplishes nothing real, nothing lasting.

Your work as a spiritual couple is your love for God made material—no less than creation was God's work of love made material. Work—true work—is, therefore, the very force of God expressed through you. It is your marriage to each other and to the universe. Sacred? Yes. But, much more than sacred. True work, like all true acts of devotion, is holy.

Take a moment and look at your hands. Take a close look at each and every finger. Notice the creases that fold around your knuckles as your fingers flex. Notice the hard nails on the end that help you pick up objects too thin for flimsy flesh alone.

Do you realize that each one of your fingers is an instrument of God's love? Each one has the power to release God's love into the world—to point our entire Garden in the direction of wholeness, health, and spiritual sanity. Our fleshly Eden cannot be redeemed without the contribution of each of your ten fingers. Without the work of your hands, Eden remains a Golden Age behind us, rather than a Golden Future ahead of us.

Tomorrow morning, after you've showered and dressed, kissed your spouse good-bye, and headed out into the traffic snarls to get to work, think about what your work really is: God's love through your hands.

And, because you are human, should you get tired or frustrated in your work, instead of throwing a childish tantrum, snap yourself back to spiritual adulthood with one question:

"Who's your boss—your *real* boss?"

If, after having worked through the lessons of these twenty-five marriage secrets, you and your partner have reached the point where you know that your only real employer is the Creator of the universe, then I've done my work well too.

EPILOGUE

Tilling the Future

. . . and at the east of the garden of Eden, he placed the cherubim,
and a sword flaming and turning
to guard the way to the tree of life.
(Genesis 3:24)

You stand there at the altar, speaking your vows to each other. But, do you realize what a marriage—a true spiritual marriage—entails? Dressed in white, with face veiled in lace, suited in a tuxedo with cheeks flushed, like a nervous schoolboy, do you realize that our entire world will be shaped through the character of your marriage, that every breath you will share as a couple shakes creation?

To what kind of marriage do you pledge yourselves? One that exists on an island? Or one that embraces the entire universe?

Returning to the Garden of Eden is a journey that every couple can make. You can achieve it quite readily, if you're willing to commit your hearts, minds, and wills to the task. The gates to the Garden are forever open. They were never shut. God never barred us from grace or excluded us from the divine presence. It is we who, in our blindness, confusion, and serpentine thinking bar ourselves from God.

Eden is not just the place for the story. Eden is, above all, a state of mind, a place, a "Where are you?" in the mind of God. Eden describes the spiritual consciousness of our true natures, made in the image and likeness of God, which we, through the challenge of physical life, are given the opportunity to uncover and discover. Therefore, Eden is not an illusion, a futile hope, or a mythical fantasy. Eden is really our true natures as human beings—the spiritual fact that we *are*. When we forget Eden, we forget ourselves. Exiled from Eden, we are exiled from true knowledge of ourselves and the goodness of life.

For those couples who accept the challenge to enter back on the road to finding Eden, there will no doubt be trials and tribulations. Until our faith and knowledge are perfected, obstacles will always appear—often in the shape of our own doubts and falsities visited back upon us through unpleasant events in our lives. If you succumb to weakness and view yourself as a victim, you will forever be downtrodden, forever be suffering while you till for thorns. But, if you realize that you, like the original couple, are in part creating your experience in the Garden through your own choices— good or evil, moral or not, aligned or un-aligned—then you are free, so very free!

These marriage secrets from the Garden were not intended to be hard-and-fast rules to be obeyed as if God were revealing unbreakable laws. They were not intended to be committed, forcibly, to memory, to become an inflexible standard by which you browbeat your spouse for every minor transgression. On the contrary, they were intended to be soft but clear guidelines to help you both make good decisions together so that you can consciously sow and reap oneness, freedom, and goodness in your life—with fewer mistakes.

If all that happens as a result of your having read this book is that you begin to hear a little whisper in your conscience reminding you to consider something bigger in your marriage than yourselves alone, then I have accomplished what I set out to achieve. If all I have done is helped you to see that your marriage is not merely personal, but *cosmic*, then I have succeeded.

This is not the same kind of Garden as the one our biblical predecessors knew. In today's Garden, we have eaten so many bites from the fruit of the Tree of Knowledge that we need computer bytes to store it all. Because of medical science, Eve no longer gives birth with such terrible labor pains. Because of industrial science, Adam no longer labors as much in the fields. In part, the curse of humanity has been lifted through the gift of our intelligence.

But, although our pain and suffering have diminished, those "punishments" remain critical lessons from God, lessons that we must never forget. They teach us that the power of life is bigger than any of us individually. They teach us that our finite individuality must always yield to the larger force of God's intention. They embed in our flesh, so that we cannot forget it, the most important lesson of all: no matter how powerful our gifts, this is not just our creation, but God's. There is an order here, one in which human beings play an important, but only a secondary, part. We are but dust.

Even if someday Adams and Eves succeed in eliminating all pain and suffering from their respective labors, can we *ever* forget the lessons God intended to teach through them? In an age of genetic re-engineering, how far shall we take our intelligence and freedom? Should we give birth to our babies in a closet, with a "grow light," like house plants, so that our right to self-expression as individuals is not compromised by the painful complications of biological parenting? What are the limits to human creativity, beyond which the very intention of God's creation is undermined?

Whose world is it, anyway?

I believe this is the critical question of today's Garden. Learning to temper our extraordinary knowledge with equally extraordinary wisdom is the only answer. It was with great foresight that God withheld the Tree of Life from us—the gift of our immortality—until we master the knowledge we stole from the Tree of Knowledge. God forbid that we should have eternal life without having had the chance to learn from our mistakes, so that we would be forced to live with their consequences forever. Our banishment to a world where there was death was the greatest of gifts to young, immature spiritual children, who had a lot of mistakes to make.

And yet today, as the length of our lives goes from seventy to eighty to ninety, and now past a hundred years of

age, it seems that our good God has even consented to dol-
ing out bites of the fruit of the Tree of Life, as well. Not
surprisingly, humanity's problems seem more and more
unsolvable, for we are living longer to see the fruit of what
we have sown. As we see our air being poisoned, we are ter-
ribly, painfully, aware of the devastating effect of our actions
upon many generations to come.

God placed every Adam and Eve in the Garden to till
the soil. But that soil was not just the meager earth. That
soil was the future—remaining to be planted, seeded in
thought, word and deed, by you! How will you succeed at
tilling the future? What kind of Garden will you create
through the work of your hands? What kind of paradise will
you bequeath to your children, and their children . . . your
offering to Eternity?

Eternal optimist that I am, I believe that at this present
moment in history we are turning the corner to a more
expansive spiritual view of the world. We are just now
beginning to see a glimmer of a world united. We are just
beginning to see the boundaries between nations dissolving, at least psychologically and economically. With technologies like the Internet, billions of human beings are
becoming a single body again—a community of "electronic
souls" communicating at the speed of light. Adam, the
original soul, also meaning "all humanity," is proving not to
be biblical metaphor, but scientific fact.

Whether we realize it or not, the world is moving *forward to Genesis*. One God, one humanity, one world—the

"socio-political platform" of the Bible, thousands of years old—still remain the only promise for our future.

How will you, as a couple, help Genesis go forward? What is the role your marriage will play in history? One thing is certain: history cannot move forward without your marriage. Indeed, your marriage—yes, yours—is the driving force of history.

What is stopping us from reclaiming paradise, here, in a real-life physical body, on a real-life physical earth, despite all our problems? Just the same temptation that confronted the biblical couple and confronts every couple:

Should we listen to the serpent and just satisfy our desires and impulses? Or should we listen to God and satisfy our desires and impulses, but in alignment to God's order?

As you stand on the altar about to pledge your lives to each other, or as you reach back into your memory, to reflect on that day perhaps decades ago—remember: your happiness, and the happiness of every creature in our Garden, depends upon your marriage and this one choice alone.

Enjoy your journey back to Eden. My wife Teddy and I are working hard at it and will be happy to meet you there.

Thanks for reading this book and, if you enjoyed it, sharing it with others.